THE

NEW WORLD ORDER

by

MAULANA MUHAMMAD 'ALI

THE AHMADIYYA ANJUMAN ISHA'AT ISLAM
LAHORE—U.S.A.

AHMADIYYA ANJUMAN ISHA'AT ISLAM LAHORE U.S.A.
P.O. Box 21328
Columbus, Ohio 43221-0328

First Edition	...	1944
Second Edition	...	1963
Third Edition	...	1984
Fourth Edition	...	1989

Library of Congress Catalog Card Number 89-085990
ISBN# 0-913221-33-8

Printed by Payette & Simms Inc.
300 Arran, Saint-Lambert
Qué J4R IK5

CONTENTS

    Preface

I.   Foundations of the New World Order   1-31

    Appendix: Summary of Islamic Teachings   32-37

II.   The Economic Problem   38-53

    Appendix: Summary of Islamic Teachings   54-58

III.   The Home   59-71

    Appendix: Summary of Islamic Teachings   72-75

IV.   The State   76-86

SOME OTHER BOOKS BY THE AUTHOR

English
- Translation of the Holy Qur'an (with commentary and Arabic text).
- Translation of the Holy Qur'an (with abridged commentary and without Arabic text).
- The Religion of Islam.
- Muhammad and Christ.
- Early Caliphate.
- Introduction to the Study of the Hadith.
- Selections from the Holy Qur'an.
- Collection and Arrangement of the Holy Qur'an.
- The Muslim Prayer Book.
- Prayers of the Holy Qur'an.
- Antichrist, Gog and Magog.
- History of the Prophets.
- The New World Order.
- A Manual of Hadith.
- Living Thoughts of the Prophet Muhammad.

Urdu
- *Bayan al-Qur'an*, translation and commentary of the Holy Qur'an, in three volumes.
- *Hama'il Sharif*, translation of the Holy Qur'an with abridged commentary.
- *Fadl al-Bari*, commentary of Sahih al-Bukhari, in 2 volumes.
- *Al-Nubuwwat fil Islam*, proof of the finality of prophethood.
- *Sirat Khair al-Bashar*, biography of the Holy Prophet.
- *Tarikh Khilafat Rashidah*, history of the first four Caliphs.
- *Maqam-i-Hadith*, the place of Tradition in Islam.
- *Zinda Nabi ki Zinda Ta'lim*, the living thoughts of the Prophet Muhammad.
- Jama' al-Qur'an, Collection and arrangement of the Qur'an.

PREFACE

Out of evil comes good, and the terrible ruin and misery of the present war may only be an inauguration of a new era of happiness for the human race. It was with such a hope that I wrote a small tract, entitled *The New World Order*, in Urdu, in December, 1942. A few months later came a suggestion, from distant Iraq, to render the same into English for the benefit of the English speaking world. This prompted me to approach the subject anew, and the present book is the result.

If the ideas presented in these pages are in any way helpful to bring about a betterment of the human race, the credit for this service to humanity does not go to the author but to the selfless and devoted band of co-workers of Ahmadiyya Anjuman Isha'at-i-Islam, Lahore who have made possible the dissemination of these ideas.

In this book, *The New World Order*, I have tried to offer a solution for the ills which materialism has brought in its train. It is a brief discussion, no doubt, but amply supported by references to original authorities. All references given without an indication of the name are to the Holy Qur'an, the first figure representing the number of the chapter and the second the number of the verse. In the references to Hadith books, *B.* stands for *Bukhari*, *M.* for *Muslim*, *Msh.* for *Mishkat*, *AD.* for *Abu Dawood*, *Tr.* for *Tirmidhi*, *Ah*, for *Musnad of Ahmad*, the two figures representing the number of the book and the number of the chapter respectively, except in the last case where reference is to volumes and pages. For a fuller discussion on most of these and other subjects relating to Islam, the reader is referred to my larger work, *The Religion of Islam*, which is a comprehensive work exhaustively dealing with the principles, laws and regulations of Islam.

Before concluding this short foreword, I must give expression of my thanks generally to every member of the

Ahmadiyya Anjuman Isha'at Islam, Lahore, who has been helpful in bringing out this work in these difficult days, and in particular to the following gentlemen who have offered liberal donations or made efforts to collect funds for the free distribution of this book on a large scale:

    M. Abdul Latif Ismail, Baghdad.
    K.S. Haji Mian Abdul Qader Patel, Bhiwandi.
    K.S. Haji Amir Sahib M. Rais, Manor.
    Syed Tasadduq Husain Qadiri, Baghdad.
    Mr. N.A. Faruqui, Bombay.
    Mirza Muzaffar Beg, Lyallpur.
    Haji S. Mian Muhammad, Lyallpur.
    Haji S. Muhammad Ismail Maula Bakhsh, Lyallpur.
    Shaikh Niaz Ahmad, Wazirabad.

Muslim Town - Lahore   MUHAMMAD 'ALI
    January 1944

1

FOUNDATIONS OF THE NEW ORDER

Humanity is to-day face to face with the biggest catastrophe and the severest crisis that it has ever seen. The devastations of the First World War were yet fresh in the minds of the present generation when, within the short space of twenty years, we find a veritable hell raging on this earth from one end to the other in the form of the Second World War. And while there is yet not the slightest indication of the subsiding of the present conflagration, there are already whispers of a Third World War; and who knows if a fourth or a fifth visitation, each more horrible than the one that precedes it, is yet in store for this world!

Are these the travails through which humanity is going to give birth to a better world order? Such is the hope of everyone who has faith in the wisdom of God; even a man who does not believe in God can see in these horrible calamities the harbinger of a mighty revolution. But, as a matter of fact, all this is happening, as will be shown later, according to a set Divine plan calculated to take humanity by gradual steps to its destined goal of perfection.

The cry of a New World Order is universal, especially in the Western world which was hitherto under the impression that by its unprecedented material advancement and unthought-of conquests of Nature it has reached the acme of perfection. That impression has received a rude shock by the happenings of the past thirty years. The material advancement, which was believed to be the source of increased happiness for the human race, has brought instead untold misery and vast destruction. The world is almost in a chaotic condition, every weak nation being the victim of the tyranny of its more powerful and more advanced neighbor. The sense of right and wrong in international relations has entirely disappeared before the passion for national aggrandizement, and this mentality rules the world from end to end. Might is as much right to-day as it was in the savage state. Instead of finding itself at the height of perfection by its great material strides, the world finds itself at the lowest depth of degradation, at the very place from which it started thousands of years ago, at the kill-and-destroy stage.

Selfishness, disregard of other's rights, indifference to moral responsibilities, tyrannising over the weak, are as rampant - perhaps more - at the height of civilization as they were in the savage state; they have only donned a different garment. Selfishness is denounced so long as it is a disease affecting one or more individuals, but when it becomes a plague and affects a whole nation, it is lauded as a great national achievement. Individuals may be secure within certain territorial limits, but whole countries are insecure and may at any time be run over by a nation which has developed a more powerful war machinery. Tyranny may not be allowed within the limits of a State, but there is nothing to check the tyranny of a nation against a nation. A certain social system may have been successful in curbing the greed of individuals, but there is nothing to curb the greed of a nation except the greater greed of a more powerful nation. Evil is taken for a virtue if it wears the cloak of nationalism. Humanity has been divided into races and nations which hate one another; in their march for advancement and their passion for more and more of material comforts and worldly pelf and power, they seek to destroy one another, not being bound by any moral code. The material civilization of the West which has made the acquisition of wealth the highest purpose of life is wholly responsible for the anarchical state of things which prevails there.

It is evident that materialism which fans the fire of human greed will bring in its trail only ruin and misery, just as it has brought in the two world wars, if there is no force to unite the human race. Such a force could only be a spiritual force. In the materially advanced Western world, the seismic centre of the convulsions which are shaking the entire world, such a moral force does not exist. Christianity which supplied such a force for centuries retreated before the advancing forces of materialism; ultimately it has been utterly routed. Its hold on Russia is now too weak to withstand the advancing tide of atheism; in Germany too, Nazism does not owe allegiance to Christianity. In most other European countries where it still lives, it lives in name only, not as a vital force. Religion is recognised only as man's private concern, and people feel ashamed of speaking of it in society. The name of God is on the lips, and the politicians, instead of serving him, requisition His services in some great national calamity or for victory in a war. God is needed more to further material gains and to serve political ends than to bring contentment of mind - as the slave of materialism, not as a spiritual force, to check the evil tendencies of materialism which are proving so ruinous for the world. Europe has practically banished God from the soil of its mind, and God has banished peace and order from the soil of Europe.

It will be said that Europe is still bent upon converting the world to Christianity; it sends out missions to and spends enormous sums of money in Asia and Africa and other parts of the world with this purpose. Does it show that Europe believes in the spiritual force of Christianity? It does not. If Europe had any faith in the spiritual value of Christianity, it should have tried to save Russia first. Europe only believes in the materialistic value of Christianity, and therefore the message of Christianity is deemed fit only for the materially backward people of the East, for the untouchables of India, for the savage Negro tribes or for the backward Chinese masses. It is thus materialism that goes about in the East wearing the cloak of Christianity. There is no sense in preaching to the East a religion which has proved spiritually an entire failure in the West itself. Christianity has not saved Europe which is now in the grip of materialism and is burning like hell from one end to the other; it is absurd to suppose that it will turn Asia into a heaven. Failure is writ large on the forehead of Christianity; its retreating forces are trying their luck in the East with the message of economic uplift, unaccompanied by any spiritual benefit.

If Christianity has any spiritual force left in it after its defeat at the hands of materialism, why does it not make an attempt to convert atheistic Russia, whose poison of godlessness is affecting the whole world, instead of sending missions to the East where belief in God still exists in greater vitality than it does in Europe and America? Europe defends itself against Russian Communism, but that too because it affects its material interests and because it is a menace to Europe's Capitalism which is the foundation-stone of European Imperialism. If Bolshevic emissaries were out only to preach godlessness and did not touch Capitalism and Imperialism of Europe, It would not move its little finger against them.

The failure of Christianity to keep the fire of faith burning in human hearts against the tide of materialism is due to two reasons. In the first place, the Christian religion - not the simple faith of Jesus Christ but as represented by the Church - was based on a dogma which was repugnant to human reason. So long as Europe was sunk low in ignorance, it remained satisfied with the authoritative Church declaration - Believe and do not question! With the advance of scientific knowledge in all branches of life, it was evident that the hold of a religion whose basic doctrines defied reason should loosen. Christianity's first clash was in fact with science. Every new discovery in the domain of science was looked upon by the Church as a heresy, because its spirit was more in consonance with ignorance than learning. It was not because of Christianity, but in spite of Christianity, that scientific research gained ground in Europe. The Church tried to suppress every scientific discovery with all the force at its command but suffered defeat every time. Then came a stage at which, contrary to all previous traditions of Christianity, reason began to be applied to Church doctrines; all basic doctrines - the Divinity of Jesus, the crucifixion, the atonement of sins, the Eucharist - when brought under the searchlight of reason, were found to have been based on the myths of ancient idolatrous nations. Christianity was the only religion known to Europe, and Jesus Christ the only God, and if these failed to satisfy the advanced mind, religion and God were bound to go along with them.

The other reason for the failure of Christianity was that it was only a creed that concerned itself with salvation in the next life. It was not a system or an order dealing with this life; all the interest that it took was in ultra-mundane questions. But with the advance of science there was a general progressive outlook of life, to which the very spirit of Christianity was opposed. The two great problems of this life, the problems of wealth and sex, as accepted by generations of Christianity, did not satisfy the advanced mind. Not only did Christianity not offer any solution to the new questions that arose in the march of civilization, it opposed all reform on these matters, and therefore men's minds were turned in disgust from it. The hold of religion on the minds of men having thus loosened, materialism remained the sole master in the field.

The cementing force of religion has thus for the time being disappeared from Europe, and the one-sided development of its civilization, the unchecked growth of materialism, has let loose the forces of selfishness, jealousy, hatred and grabbing political power, which have brought ruin and destruction upon humanity. The first requisite of the New World Order, therefore, is that it must be based on *spiritual force* which religion alone can supply. If the foundations are not deep and reliable, the superstructure of the New Order would go to pieces. This is what happened twenty years ago. The First World War raged for over four years, visiting ruin and desolation on populous cities and towns, changing fertile lands into barren wastes, killing hundreds of thousands of the healthiest youth, maiming even greater numbers for their lives, destroying the happiness of millions of homes, and plunging vast sections of humanity into misery and affliction. The end of the war seemed to justify all these sacrifices. The aggressor was defeated, and the democracies won a complete victory. There were summoned together the best brains from the winning nations and a great international conference was convened so as to lay the foundations of a New World Order. The map of Europe was redrawn. New territorial bounds were demarcated. The vanquished aggressors were so cut up into pieces that never again should they regain the strength to raise their heads. The League of Nations was created to give this Order a moral support. This was New World Order No.1.

Where is that Order to-day? It went to pieces within ten years of its creation, and another ten plunged the world into a conflagration more horrible than the first. All the travail that humanity had to go through ended in smoke. Why? Because the New Order had no moral foundations. The worthy people that assembled at the conference gave no thought to the real ills of humanity. They thought that vanquishment of one nation by another was a remedy for future aggression. It was not, and it shall never be. They did nothing to eliminate the mutual hatred of the warring factions. They did nothing to bring about a change of heart, either in the conquerors or in the conquered. They did not pay the least attention to the fact that in their peace proposals they were only giving impetus to the very human greed which had brought about the great disaster. They talked of everything excepting how to weld humanity into one nation, and how to lay a moral foundation for the superstructure of their New Order. The proposed moral support of the League of Nations was nothing but a farce; it was rightly called a League of Thieves by Iqbal, because each one of them had but one desire in his heart of hearts: how to steal away material advantages for his own nation; and not one of them was inspired by the noble idea: how to weld the different nations into one humanity.

Now we are in the midst of the Second World War and the vanquishment of the aggressors is again in sight. All kinds of questions are being discussed as to what World Order No. 2 should be, but one question is again conspicuous by its absence: how are the different nations to be welded into one humanity? If this question is not tackled seriously, this new offering at the altar of the god of war in the shape of untold human woe and misery and the devastation of civilisation will go in vain, and World Order No. 2 will go the way of World Order No. 1. It will only pave the way for another and perhaps more terrific world cataclysm. No conference of materialistic people, no league of greedy nations, can bring salvation to Europe. The solution of a thousand materialistic questions will not bring peace unless the moral foundation for welding different nations into one humanity, and for a change of greedy mentality, is discovered first. The way the politicians are going is not the way of the Kingdom of God, and peace will only come to humanity when the Kingdom of God is established on earth. World Order No. 2, if based on the same materialistic foundations of how to divide the booty, will surely lead to World War No. 3 as World Order No. 1 has led to World War No. 2.

It is the greatest misfortune of humanity that religion which alone can furnish the moral foundations on which a true World Order can be established has been put under taboo, and the very panacea is deemed to be a poison. Hatred of religion has become the fashion among the materially advanced people, without giving a thought to the incontrovertible fact that religion has been the supreme force in the development of mankind to its present condition. As a matter of fact, human civilisation as we have it to-day, is based on religion. Religion has made possible a state of civilisation which has again and again saved human society from disruption. Trace back the history of human civilisation among all nations, and it will be seen that whenever it has begun to totter, a new religious impulse has always been at hand to save it from utter destruction. It is not only that civilisation, with any pretence to endurance, can rest only on a moral basis, and that true and lofty morals are inspired only by faith in God, even the unity and cohesion of jarring human elements, without which it is impossible for any human civilisation to stand for a day, is best brought about by the unifying force of religion.

It is often said that religion is responsible for much of the hatred and bloodshed in the world, but a cursory glance at the history of religion will show this to be a monstrous misconception. Love, concord, sympathy, kindness to one's fellow-men, has been the message of every religion, and every nation has learnt these essential lessons in their true purity only through the spirit of selflessness and service which faith in God has inspired. If there have been selfishness and hatred and bloodshed among religious people, they have been there in spite of religion, not as a consequence of the message of love which religion has brought. They have been there because human nature is too prone to these things; and their presence only shows that a still greater religious awakening is required, that a truer faith in God is yet a crying need of humanity. That men shall sometimes turn to low and unworthy things does not show that the nobler sentiments are worthless; it only shows that their development has become all the more an urgent need.

If unification be the true basis of human civilisation, by which phrase I mean the civilisation, not of one nation or of one country, but of humanity as a whole, then Islam is undoubtedly the greatest civilising force the world has ever known or is likely to know. Thirteen hundred years ago, it was Islam that saved it from crushing into an abyss of savagery, that came to the help of a civilisation whose very foundations had collapsed, and that set about laying new foundations and rearing an entirely new edifice of culture and ethics. A new idea of the unity of the human race as a whole, not of the unity of this or that nation, was introduced into the world; an idea so mighty that it welded together nations which had warred with and hated one another since the world began. It was not only in Arabia, among the ever-fighting tribes of a single peninsula, that this great miracle, as an English writer calls it, was wrought, a miracle before the magnitude of which everything dwindles into insignificance:

"A more disunited people it would be hard to find till suddenly the miracle took place. A man arose who, by his personality and by his claim to direct Divine guidance, actually brought about the impossible - namely the union of all these warring factions."[1]

It not only cemented together the warring tribes of one country but it established a brotherhood of all the nations of the world, joining together even those which had nothing in common except their common humanity. It obliterated differences of colour, race, language, geographical boundaries and even differences of culture. It united man with man as such, and the hearts of those in the far east began to beat in unison with the hearts of those in the farthest west. Indeed it proved to be not only the greatest but the only force uniting humanity, because whereas other religions had succeeded merely in unifying the different elements of a single race or a single nation, Islam actually achieved the unification of different races

---

1. The Ins and Outs of Mesopotamia, p. 99.

and nations, and harmonised the jarring and discordant elements of humanity.

Islam not only made the different human races a single race but united different nations into a single human nation. Upon this basis, the surest basis of civilisation, it brought back to man his lost civilisation. Thus writes J.H. Denison in *Emotion as the Basis of Civilization*:
"In the fifth and sixth centuries, the civilized world stood on the verge of chaos. The old emotional cultures that had made civilization possible, since they had given to men a sense of unity and of reverence for their rulers, had broken down, and nothing had been found adequate to take their place....

"It seemed then the great civilization which it had taken four thousand years to construct was on the verge of disintegration, and that mankind was likely to return to that condition of barbarism where every tribe and sect was against the next, and law and order were unknown....The old tribal sanctions had lost their power....The new sanctions created by Christianity were working division and destruction instead of unity and order....Civilization like a gigantic tree whose foliage had overreached the world....stood tottering....rotted to the core....Was there any emotional culture that could be brought in to gather mankind once more into unity and to save civilization?"

And then speaking of Arabia:
"It was among these people that the man was born who was to unite the whole known world of the east and south."

Civilisation is once more faced with disintegration and destruction owing to a condition similar to that prevailing in the sixth century. Nation has risen against nation, seeking to destroy one another. Some force is needed - and that is the first need of humanity to-day- which should unite the different nations into one humanity. This force which should bring about a change of mentality so as to eliminate mutual jealousies and hatred can only be a moral force, and a moral force can be supplied only by religion. Islam supplied such a force in the seventh century beginning with Arabia. In those days Arabia presented a scene of internecine warfare exactly similar to that which Europe presents to-day. Tribes and clans that inhabited that desert-land were in the grip of unending feuds. The smallest thing served as a matchstick to set ablaze the flames of war which lasted for years. All the tribes would plunge themselves into the conflagration, some ranging themselves on one side, some on the other. There was wholesale bloodshed and destruction. After exhausting themselves they would conclude peace. Hardly would the ink of the treaty dry up when old grudges which kept smouldering would burst up and once more the country would find itself in the flames of war. Thus went on things for long generations from sire to son and from son to grandson. The whole people were on the verge of being consumed to ashes by these flames of warfare, when, lo! God in His mercy poured down from above the cooling waters which once for all extinguished the last embers of those age-long enmities and grudges, replacing them by mutual sympathy and affection.

Strange as it might appear, the brotherhood of which the basis was laid in Arabia in the seventh century was not limited to that peninsula. Within a century, vast territories beyond the boundaries of Arabia received the light of learning and civilisation which was established in that little known peninsula. The unification of humanity which was the foundation-stone of this new culture was unique, and the world had not seen the like of it before. No other reformer or religion had ever dreamed of such a brotherhood of man - a brotherhood which knew no bounds of colour, race, country, language or even of rank; a unity of the human race beyond which conception cannot go. It not only recognizes the equality of the civil and political rights of men, but also that of their spiritual rights. "Mankind is a single nation" (2:213) is its fundamental doctrine, and for that reason every nation is recognised having received the spiritual gift of revelation, which up to this time had only been conceived as a gift to this or that favoured nation. "And there is not a people but a warner has gone among them" (35:24).

The conception of humanity as one nation, notwithstanding the diversity of races and colours and languages and outstepping all geographical boundaries, is Islam's unique contribution to human civilisation. It is the only panacea for the poison of national jealousies and hatred which has brought humanity, along with its civilisation, to the verge of destruction. Christianity is, like Islam, an international religion in the sense that it embraces various nations in its fold, but, in the real sense of the word, in bringing all nations to one level and in bringing about harmony among these nations, Islam is the only international religion. In this respect Christianity has been a signal failure. Christians of white colour to this day hate Christians of black colour though living in the same country, as in the case of America, the most advanced Christian country and the home of democracy, where, in spite of the pious wishes of Mr. Roosevelt, the Negro and the white man cannot gather together under one roof. Christians of the West still consider themselves superior to Christians of the East, who cannot worship God in the same church with them. Christian converts from among the low castes in India are still untouchables in the eyes of converts to Christianity from among the high-caste Hindus. Christianity has hopelessly failed in bringing about unification of humanity. Islam, on the other hand, has given birth to a World Order of universal brotherhood in which the Western and Eastern, the white and the black, the Aryan and the Semitic, the Indian and the Negro, stand on the same level. The moment a Negro or an untouchable enters the fold of Islam, he assumes a position of equality in all respects with the white or the high-caste convert to Islam, with every member of the Muslim brotherhood, in fact. He can not only worship in the same mosque but can stand shoulder to shoulder with the noblest of his brethren, and can dine sitting on the same table with him. Islam's levelling and harmonising influence is not known to any other religion or society or order in the world.

The real world-democracy, which signifies an equality of status for all human beings as such, can be attained only through Islam. It possesses such a mighty spiritual influence that as soon as a man joins this Order, he feels himself raised to a high level where all distinctions of race, colour, caste and rank disappear as if by a magic wand. That Islam possesses this spiritual power even to-day, notwithstanding the loss of its temporal power, is admitted by both, friend and foe. Here is the concluding para of Gibb's *Whither Islam* (p.379):

"But Islam has yet a further service to render to the cause of humanity....No other society has such a record of success in uniting in an equality of status, of opportunity, and of endeavour so many and so various races of mankind. The great Muslim communities of Africa, India and Indonesia, perhaps also the small Muslim communities in China and the still smaller community in Japan, show that Islam has still the power to reconcile apparently irreconcilable elements of race and tradition. If ever the opposition of the great societies of the East and West is to be replaced by co-operation, the mediation of Islam is an indispensable condition."

What is the secret of Islam's success in establishing a world brotherhood and in bringing about unification of different nations? In the first place, the basic teaching of Islam is that the whole human race is a single family, with God as its creator, and its division into different branches and tribes is only meant to make people know each other better: "O mankind, We have created you from a male and a female, and made you tribes and families that you may know each other. Surely the noblest of you with Allah is most dutiful of you" (49:13). And just as in individuals, so among nations. The superior nation is not that which reduces others to slavery and tramples their rights under its feet; morally such a nation is on the lower plane of a savage nation. The superior nation - the one honourable with God - is that which honours the rights of others. A Muslim's conception of humanity, therefore, is that it is but one family, whatever differences there may be in colours and languages and cultures, with God as the Lord or, in Christian terminology, the Father of all. Members of one family may quarrel with one another now and then, but they cannot hate one another for ever. In fact, this broad conception of humanity is the only safeguard against national, racial or colour prejudices, and only on this basis can peace be established on this earth.

Secondly, the basic idea of the equality and fraternity of all men is worked into practice in a Muslim's life by the institution of prayer. All Muslims gather together daily in mosques to offer prayers, where they all stand before their Maker shoulder to shoulder, the king along with his poorest subject, the rich arrayed in gorgeous robes with the beggar clad in rags, the white man with the black. Differences of rank, wealth and colour vanish inside the mosque, and quite a new atmosphere, an atmosphere of brotherhood, equality and love, differing totally from the outside world, prevails within the holy precincts. To be able to breathe five times daily in an atmosphere of perfect peace in a world of strife and struggle, of equality where inequality is the order of the day, and of love amid the petty jealousies and enmities of daily life, is a great blessing. Man has to work in his daily life amidst inequalities, amidst strife and struggle, amidst scenes of hatred and enmity; he is drawn out of these five times a day, and made to realise that equality, fraternity and love are the real sources of human happiness. Even if we do not take into account the great advantage which a man gains by feeling himself in the Divine presence in the mosque, the time spent in prayer is not wasted from the point of view of active humanitarianism. On the contrary, the best use of it is made in learning those great lessons which make life worth living. And these lessons of fraternity, equality and love, when put into practice in daily life, serve as foundations for the unification of the human race and of the lasting civilisation of mankind. In fact, the five daily congregational prayers are meant, among other things, to carry into practice the theoretical lessons of equality and fraternity for which Islam stands; and however much Islam may have preached in words the equality of man and the fraternity of the community of Islam, all this would have remained a dead letter, had it not been translated into the everyday life of man through the institution of the daily congregational prayers.

At the same time prayer serves another great end. The object of religion is not merely to preach the doctrine of the existence of God as a theory; it goes far beyond that. Religion seeks to instil the conviction that God is a living force in the life of man, and prayer is the means by which it is sought to achieve this great end. The real conviction that *God is* comes to man, not by the belief that there is a God in the outer world, but by the realisation of the Divine within himself, and this realisation is attained through prayer. The universal experience of humanity bears out the truth of this. In every age and among every nation there have been men who, through prayer, have realised the great truth of Divine existence within their hearts, and have laid down their lives for the good of humanity. In their case, belief in the existence of God was a moral force which not only worked an entire change in their own lives, but also enabled them to transform the entire lives of nations for centuries and changed the histories of peoples and countries. Their selflessness and truthfulness were beyond reproach, and their testimony, which is the testimony of all nations in all ages, establishes the one fact that belief in the existence of God becomes a moral force of the first magnitude when once it is realised in the heart of man through prayer to the Divine Being. So great a moral force it is, indeed, that even the most powerful material forces give way before it. Is not the experience of these great personalities a beacon light for others, showing them that they also can make God a moral force in their lives? The powers and faculties that are given to one man are also given to another, and through their proper use one man can do what another before him has done.

In fact, civilisation does not rest on the material comforts which man has gained through conquest of Nature. Its real foundations are the noble sentiments which faith in God inspires. A cursory glance at the history of human civilization will show that faith in God has been the supreme force in the development of mankind to its present condition. That all that is noble and good in man is not due to man's conquest of Nature but to his conquest of self, inspired by faith in God, is a truth which no one can deny. It is men like Abraham, Moses, Christ, Buddha, Krishna, Confucius and Muhammad who have changed the history of the human race, and raised it from the depths of degradation to moral heights. It is through the teachings and example of this or that prophet that man has been able to conquer his lower nature, and to set before himself the noble ideals of selflessness and service of humanity. Study the noble sentiments that inspire man to-day and you will find their origin in the teachings and example of some great sage who had a deep faith in God, and through whom was sown the seed of faith in other human hearts. The moral and ethical development of man to his present state, which alone in a real sense can be called the civilisation of man - the material gains are only a secondary thing - is due to faith. To all appearance, the reign of materialism must needs entail the rule of selfishness. A cut-and-dried scheme for the equal division of wealth will never inspire the noble sentiments which are to-day the pride of man. Godlessness will make the masses sink back, gradually of course, into the state of barbarism.

In fact, a stable human civilisation can stand only on two pillars: faith in God and unity of man. The materialism which is to-day prevailing in Europe has pulled down both these pillars, and unless they are restored again, Europe, with all its material comforts, can never have access to true happiness of the heart or to peace among the nations. And just as Islam is the only order known to this world that has been successful in establishing a world brotherhood and in welding the different nations into one nation, it is the only religion which has succeeded in keeping the spirit of man in contact with the Divine spirit, withstanding the forces of materialism. It is a fact that Muslims as a nation have more vital faith in God than the followers of any other religion. It is this faith in God that accounts for the early Muslim conquests which are unparalleled in the history of the world. So far as material resources were concerned, Persia and Rome had abundance of them and the Arabs were poor in this respect. The war machinery of the former was far more powerful; in numbers too the Arabs could not bear any comparison with the fighting forces of these two empires. Yet when these mighty empires came into clash with Muslim Arabia - and they were the aggressors - they were swept away like a straw before the mighty spiritual force of Islam, the Muslim's faith in God and in the justness of his cause. It was this same faith in God that enabled Muslims to hold their own against the onslaughts of Christian Europe during the Crusades. It is this same faith in God again that enables Muslims to-day to carry on the contest with Christianity for the mastery of the world, in spite of the fact that all material forces in this contest - wealth, power and organisation - are on the side of Christianity. The Islamic institution of prayer which keeps the spirit of the Muslim in touch with the divine spirit is without doubt the basis on which this strong faith in God rests, and the value of prayer in the formation of this noble trait in the Muslim national character is incalculable. As every Muslim feels himself in the august Divine presence five times a day, faith in God sways his mentality even in his outlook on the material world, and thus becomes a living force in his life.

Islam can thus supply to Europe the two great moral forces - a *living faith in God* and *an order based on the oneness of humanity* - which can restore peace to it. Unless European society is willing to receive these two heavenly gifts from Islam, its disasters will not end. Let Europe diagnose its disease with a cool mind and apply the remedy with a brave heart. Let it not repeat the mistake of earlier days and look upon its real friend as its foe. Europe sought to destroy Islam with the sword in the Crusades, but it failed. The opposition after this has taken a subtler turn. Not only did the European soldier go back to his home filled with the false conviction that Islam was Europe's enemy, and a frightful one, because he met him only on the battlefield, and that conviction was left as an inheritance from sire to son, but also Europe's leaders in political and religious thought - past masters in the art of propaganda - augmented this hatred by drawing a picture of Islam which was the very opposite of reality. Islam was, in the truest sense of the word, a message of *peace* for the whole world, the most tolerant religion which had ever been preached, but it was misrepresented as the most tyrannical and intolerant faith. Islam not only recognised in the clearest words the Divine origin of all the great religious systems of the world, laying it down that there was not a single nation on the face of this earth to which a warner or a guide had not been sent to draw it closer to God[2]; it went further and required everyone who entered the fold of Islam to believe in the prophets of all other nations, just as he believed in the Prophet of Islam.[3] But the political and religious leaders of Europe actually drew a picture of the Prophet Muhammad as going about with the sword in one hand and the Qur'an in the other. And notwithstanding the clear light that has

---

2. "And there is not a people but a warner has gone among them" (35:24).

"And for every nation there is a messenger" (10:47).

"And every people had a guide" (13:7).

3. "And who believe in that which has been revealed to thee and that which was revealed before thee" (2:4).

been thrown on these topics recently, European writers still represent Islam to be the religion of the sword.[4]

Under a most unfortunate misconception Europe sought to destroy Islam by weakening it politically on the one hand, and carrying on, on the other, false and abusive propaganda against it in the religious field. If there was anything on which the whole of Europe was agreed, it was that Islam was Europe's greatest enemy and that it must be destroyed or weakened, by fair means or foul. The politician and the missionary, to whatever nation they belonged, worked conjointly to this end. Almighty God, in His wisdom, had, however, ordained otherwise. Islam was a blessing for humanity and it had to be spared. The European nations, among which real harmony had never existed, became jealous of each other, and this jealousy ultimately developed, as it was bound to do, into the severest hatred and enmity, and the urge to destroy each other has taken the place of the urge to destroy Islam. Christendom's sin of seeking to destroy its real friend had been visited with a corresponding punishment: the destruction of mutual friendly relations and the desire to destroy each other. This is in accordance with the Divine plan announced thirteen hundred years ago:

"And with those who say, We are Christians, We made a covenant, but they neglected a portion of that they were reminded; so *We stirred up enmity and hatred among them to the day of Resurrection.* And Allah will soon inform them of what they did. O People of the Book, indeed, Our Messenger has come to you, making clear to you much of that which you concealed of the Book and passing over much. Indeed, there has come to you from Allah, a light and a clear Book, whereby Allah *guides* such as follow His pleasure *into the ways of peace*, and brings them out of darkness into light by His will, and guides

---

4. "The spread of Islam by arms is a religious duty upon Muslims in general" (D.B. Macdonald, *Encyclopaedia of Islam*, Art. "Djihad").

them to the right path...O people of the Book, indeed Our Messenger has come to you explaining to you after a cessation of the messengers, lest you say: There came not to us a bearer of good news nor a warner. So indeed a bearer of good news and a warner has come to you" (5:14-19).

The convenant spoken of in the first verse quoted above is in reference to the prophecies of the advent of the Holy Prophet Muhammad to be met with in the Gospels, and Jesus Christ's order to his followers to accept the great Prophet with whose advent a perfect World Order will be revealed to humanity.[5] We are further told, in the verses quoted above, that real peace would come to Christendom only when it accepts the World Order established by Islam.

That the great civilisation of Europe should work its own destruction because of its one-sided growth is also a part of the Divine plan revealed through the Holy Prophet Muhammad, peace and blessings of Allah be upon him, the

---

5. In this connection I may quote only one prophecy here:

"I have yet many things to say unto you, but ye cannot bear them now. Howbeit when he, the spirit of truth, is come, he will guide you into all truth: .... He shall glorify me"(John 16:12-14). Jesus Christ was sent only as a reformer for the Israelites and he denounced only their crying evils. But the Spirit of Truth - the advent of the Holy Prophet is spoken of as the coming of *the Truth* in the Holy Qur'an (17:81) - was to guide men into *all truth*, showing that the Order to be revealed to him would be perfect. There is no other Law in the world except Islam which claims perfection: "This day have I perfected for you your religion" (5:3). The Prophet Muhammad did glorify Jesus inasmuch as it was he who cleared him and his mother of all those charges which his own people, the Israelites, preferred against him, and also because it was he who established his true position as a man-prophet.

materialism of Europe finding express mention in the Holy Qur'an:

"Say, Shall We inform you who are the greatest losers in the respect of deeds? Those whose effort goes astray in this world's life, and they think that they are making good manufactures. Those are they who disbelieve in the messages of their Lord and meeting with Him, so their works are vain. Nor shall we set up a balance for them on the day of Resurrection. That is their reward - hell, because they disbelieved and held My messages and My messengers in mockery" (18:103-106).

Here is an exact description of the civilisation of the West, of the pride of Christendom: *all effort lost in this world's life - manufacture being its great speciality - and utter loss of God-vision.* So far as worldly gains are concerned, its star is in the ascendance, and looks the brightest; as regards matters spiritual, its eye is closed.[6] The portrait of modern civilisation attains to most vivid clearness in the above verses.[7] Manufacture is the one speciality and pride of the West; but, we are told, these people would be so engrossed in the race of manufacturing goods that they would have no thought of God left in their minds. They would therefore lose that peace of mind which God-vision alone can give. They would have too thick scales on their eyes to see beyond their little

---

6. The vision of Christ, after whom Christianity goes in name only - in spirit it is the negation of what he taught - was entirely different. He cared not for things of this life and cared only to bring God-vision to this world. So far as the spirit is concerned, present Christianity is Antichrist. In one of the sayings of the Holy Prophet Muhammad the Antichrist is described as having the right - the spiritual - eye quite closed, and the left - the material - eye shining like a bright star. This is a most beautiful figurative description of the Western civilisation.

7. These verses are, according to Hadith, an antidote for the Antichrist.

manufactures and have a glimpse of the blissful glory of God. The passion for production and possession would so seize upon them that it would make them oblivious of all higher values of life. Production and more production, possession and more possession - this would be the be-all and the end-all of life with them. Whole nations would be engrossed in these pursuits, and in these they would strive to outstrip one another. At long last, however, these very manufactures of theirs would prove their undoing. Their hearts would prove their undoing. Their hearts would get filled with mutual hatred, and they would be out, day and night, planning and counterplanning, to encompass the destruction of one another.

This destruction of the materialistic civilisation of the West is still more explicitly mentioned in the beginning of the 18th Chapter - *The Cave* - which deals with the history of Christianity, the verses quoted above occurring towards the end of it:
"And to warn those who say: Allah has taken a son. They have no knowledge of it, nor had their fathers. Grievous is the word that comes out of their mouths. . . . Then may be thou wilt kill thyself with grief, sorrowing after them, if they believe not in this announcement. Surely, We have made whatever is on the earth an embellishment for it, so that We may try which of them is best in works. And We will surely make what is on it dust, without herbage" (18:4-8).[8]

The first verse shows that it is the Christian nations that are being spoken of here; the last two show that these nations will beautify the earth with their conquest of Nature, but that all this, because of their own misdeeds, will come to ruin, and the beautiful cities raised on it will be razed to the ground and great gardens turned into wasteland.

---

8. According to Hadith, these verses furnish the key as to what the tribulation of the Antichrist is.

Elsewhere it is stated that this devastation of civilisation will be so wide as to cover the whole earth, not a town will remain that will not have a taste of this ruin:

"And there is not a town but We will destroy it before the day of Resurrection or chastise it with a severe chastisement. That is written in the Book" (17:58).

We are further told that the sentence of punishment which will be brought down on these nations as a consequence of their great sin in rejecting the peace which Islam offers, nay in seeking to destroy this Divine Message of Peace, will be executed through these nations themselves. Europe will be the instrument through which Europe's ruin will be worked. Providence sometimes appoints one people to punish another. The Jews were punished for their transgressions at the hands of Nebuchadnezzar. The Muslims were visited with Divine punishment at the hands of Hulagu, when Baghdad, the centre of Muslim civilisation, was razed to the ground. Europe was too powerful to be punished by another people; she is made to suffer torture for her evil deeds at her own hands. This part of the Divine scheme is also made clear in the Holy Qur'an, where European nations are spoken of under the name of Gog and Magog[9]: "When Gog and

---

9. Gog and Magog are spoken of as taking a servant of God for God (18:99-104) which is the Qur'anic description of the Christians. On another occasion too, the mention of Gog and Magog follows the mention of Jesus (21:91-96). The Bible speaks of Gog and Magog as residing to the north of Caucasus: "Son of man, set thy face against Gog, the land of Magog, the chief prince of Meshech and Tubal, and prophesy against him. And say, Thus saith the Lord God, Behold I *am* against thee, O Gog, the chief prince Meshech and Tubal" (Ezek. 38:2-3). "And I will send a fire on Magog, and among them that dwell carelessly in the isles: and they shall know that I *am* the Lord" (Ezek. 39:6). Gog is here spoken of as the chief prince of Meshech and Tubal, and north of the Caucasus we still find two rivers

Magog are made to overcome the world and they shall break forth from every elevated place" (21:96). In Hadith, Gog and Magog are described as powerful nations which would overcome the world, and with whom "no people of the world will have the power to fight" (*Muslim*).

In the case of these nations, transgression was therefore to be punished by making some of them rise against others. Here again the Holy Qur'an is clear:
"And on that day We shall let some of them surge against others" (18:99).

And again:
"And We shall bring forth hell, exposed to view, on that day before the disbelievers" (18:100).

This is what we actually find. European people first fell upon foreign lands and subjugated the weaker nations. No nation of the world had the might to withstand them. After having overcome almost the whole world, they rushed at and fell in deadly grips with one another. They have themselves become the instruments of ruining what they built with their own hands. The hell that is spoken of in the above verses as being the result of their mutual conflict is raging to-day, not only in Europe but more or less throughout the world. God deals justly by His creatures, and this hell in this world has been made

---

bearing names corresponding to these Biblical names, i.e., Moskoa and Tubal, on the former of which is situated the ancient city of Moscow and on the latter the more recent town of Tobolsk. The prophecies of the Bible thus point to Europe as the threatened land. In the Urdu, Arabic and Persian versions, translated from Hebrew, the words of Ezek. 38:2 are: "the chief prince of Rus, Meshech and Tubal," Rus being the Arabic and Persian name for Russia. The presence of the effigies of Gog and Magog in Guildhall, London, from very early times is also a point worth considering.

manifest because men would not mind God's Reminder, would not even lend their ears to any such talk:
"These are the people whose eyes were under a cover from My Reminder, and they could not bear to hear" (18:101).

According to the Holy Qur'an, however, all chastisement is corrective:
"And We sent (messengers) to nations before thee, then We seized them with distress and affliction that they might humble themselves" (6:42).

The travails of the world are not in vain. Out of affliction comes real happiness. Evolution is working not only physically but also spiritually.

In the very first verse of the Holy Qur'an, the one most repeated, God is spoken of as Rabb al-'alamin. The word *Rabb* means *fostering of a thing in such a manner as to make it attain one condition after another until it reaches its goal of completion*, and 'alamin means *worlds* or *nations*. Hence God, according to Islam, is *Nourisher unto perfection* of mankind, *of all the nations*. The world is moving on towards advancement by steps and stages. And the present worldwide disaster, the heaviest ruin that has ever visited this earth, may move the world on by the largest stride. Speaking of the great conflict of European nations, the Holy Qur'an says:
"And the trumpet will be blown, then We shall gather them all together" (18:99).

The blowing of the trumpet indicates the coming of a mighty revolution. The unification of the fighting nations into *one nation* is a broad enough hint at the nation of Islam; for there is but one faith, Islam, which has been able to weld different nations into one homogeneous whole; and this, therefore, is the New World Order on which depends the advancement of man towards a higher goal.

As already shown, Islam was successful in bringing about a unification of the dissentient elements of humanity through Divine service, i.e., by deepening the roots of God-consciousness in human heart. And though faith in God and faith in the oneness of humanity must remain the two foundations of any World Order that could subsist and save humanity from disaster and restore to it peace of mind, yet even the oneness of humanity is only a corollary of vital faith in God, and therefore faith in God is the real foundation. The torch of this faith is kept burning by the God-consciousness which is awakened in the human heart by the Islamic institution of prayer. Islam does not allow that God-consciousness which is implanted in the very nature of man, should lie dormant for six days in the week and the receive a stirring up on the seventh. It is a fire which can be kept live only if stirred every now and then.

Prayer is, therefore, a part of the everyday affairs of man. There is a prayer in the morning when rising from the bed - man's first daily work - and a prayer in the night when going to bed - his last daily work; and in the midst of these there are other prayers during hours of business or recreation. This is the Islamic arrangement: to call back a man when he is in the midst of his worldly engagements and to usher him into the Divine presence; to awaken in him, in the midst of all his turmoils and agitations which are likely to lead away his mind from God, the consciousness that there is a Higher Presence to Whom he is really responsible for every act; to remind him in the hour of triumph that he is nothing but a weak and humble creature of God, and in the hour of his failure and disappointment that he has still a support to fall back upon, and that there is nothing to despair of. Prayer thus not only awakens God-consciousness in man; it adds a new zeal to his work, to which he goes back with a fresh mind.

What is the prayer which Islam teaches? It gives the individual full freedom to ask from God for anything that he needs and to give vent to his feelings in the presence of his Maker as He likes, but at the same time it directs him to seek in the first place guidance from the All-Knowing, All-Powerful God. The Muslim's most important prayer is that contained in the Opening Chapter of the Holy Qur'an, a prayer which he generally offers five times a day:

"Thee do we serve, (O our Nourisher unto perfection!) and Thee do we ask for help, Guide us on the right path. The path of those on whom Thou hast bestowed favours" (1:4-6).

In the first place, this prayer creates in man the mentality to "serve God," to obey the Divine commandments even when they are opposed to his own wishes, or to the requirements of his environment, or to the usages and traditions of the people among whom he lives. Secondly, it creates the mental attitude not to despair in the greatest difficulties and to seek strength, when all means have failed, from the Source of all strength. The man who depends on the help of God knows no despair, and has the strength to withstand the hardest trials.

The most important part of this prayer, however, is that in which man is taught to seek guidance from God in all his affairs. The Muslim's God does not live on his lips; He lives in the deepest depths of his heart. He seeks help from Him hourly, and he seeks guidance from him in whatever he undertakes. If one does not believe in a guiding God, one does not believe in Him at all. Are we not in the midst of difficulties every now and then? Is there not darkness around us momently? Who can show us light in the midst of darkness? It is only God. The man is morally armed who seeks guidance from God in all his affairs, and this is what prayer in Islam means.

Prayer is an expression of the soul's inmost desire, and the desire that Islam seeks to create in the human heart is to be guided in the right path, to be led on and on to the great goal of life. It makes the soul aspire to the highest eminence. The Muslim's attitude towards the world is not one of inaction or listlessness; it is one of continuous struggle to be led on and on until he attains to perfection. He gives praise to God at every step, cries out *al-hamdulillah* (*all praise is due to God*), and the mentality thus created is to live in perfect peace with his environment. Yet he is not in a stationary condition. Nor is he the slave of his environment; he struggles and strives throughout his life to master it. He does not stand for peace without progress, nor yet for progress without peace, but for peace and progress combined. The mentality thus created in the individual ultimately becomes a national characteristic, for individuals make a nation; and when the same mentality is created in all the individuals of a nation, it becomes the nation's mentality. If one wants to see what change Islam can bring about, one should only study the all-round progress that the earlier Muslim generations made in the world.

Prayer, however, is not the only means through which Islam keeps faith alive in the heart of man, and thus makes religion a vital force in his life. There is also the Divine arrangement which is peculiar to Islam that there appear in it from time to time men of a higher God-consciousness who draw their fellow-beings closer to God and revive faith in Him. The followers of all religions believe that God spoke to some great sage or sages of the past; but Islam alone, of all the religions of the world, teaches that God speaks to the elect even now as He spoke in the past. The question naturally arises: if God listens to prayers as He listened in the past, how is it that He does not speak now as He spoke in the past? Therefore, though revelation was made perfect and prophethood came to a close in the person of the Holy Prophet Muhammad, it does not mean that God has ceased to speak after that. He speaks to the elect even now, because speaking is one of His attributes, and Divine attributes never cease to function. Prophets are not raised now because the Law was made perfect with the advent of the Holy Prophet

Muhammad; but revelation and prophethood are two different things, and it is an error to confuse the discontinuance of prophethood with the discontinuance of revelation. Revelation in its lower forms is common to both prophets and those that are not prophets; it is only the highest form of revelation which is peculiar to the prophets.

This is, in fact, the reason why faith in God has ceased to be a vital force except in Islam. That God revealed Himself and spoke to a man thousands of years ago, and that is not the universal experience of humanity, deprives faith in God of all vitality. In fact, God and religion are thus dismissed as things of the past, and Revelation becomes a story with no living force. Islam universalises revelation and establishes it on a scientific basis. Revelation, in the first place, according to the Holy Qur'an, is not the solitary experience of this or that nation but the universal experience of humanity. The elect to whom God spoke and revealed Himself appeared among all nations and in all ages, and revelation is thus the experience of the whole human race. And, secondly, Islam teaches that revelation is still a fact and God still speaks to His elect. Such elect are even now needed to impart vitality to faith in God; but they are not called prophets because they do not bring a new law, nor do they make any changes in the existing law.

In fact, the finality of prophethood was a need without which the unification of humanity was impossible. Every nation had its prophet; and thus, though prophethood was in one sense a universal fact, prophets appearing in every nation, it was more or less a national institution, the scope of the teachings of every prophet being limited to his own nation. National prophethood cemented the bonds of national unity; but the time was fast approaching when international unity or world unity would be needed, and this could be effected only by sending a world-prophet, or one prophet to all the nations of the world. Only thus could the grand idea of unifying the whole human race be brought to perfection. The Holy Prophet Muhammad's mission is thus described in the Holy Qur'an:

"Blessed is He Who sent down the Discrimination upon His servant that he might be a warner to the nations" (25:1):

"Say: O mankind, surely I am the Messenger of Allah to you all, of Him, Whose is the kingdom of the heavens and the earth" (7:158).

"And We have not sent thee but as a bearer of good news and as warner to all mankind" (34:28).

"And We have not sent thee but as a mercy to the nations" (21:107).

The Prophet Muhammad was a prophet of God like any other prophet, but his advent marked a revolution in the history of prophethood. The day of the national prophet came to an end, and a new day dawned upon the world with the world-prophet who was to combine the different nations into one nation. The grand idea of unifying the whole human race, and gathering it together under one banner, was thus brought to perfection. All geographical limitations were swept away as were all bars of colour and race, and the basis of the unity of the human race was laid upon the grand principle that the whole human race was one, and that all men, wherever they may be found, were a single nation. Such unity could not be accomplished unless the finality of prophethood was established; for, if prophets continued to appear after the world-prophet, they would undoubtedly demand the allegiance of this or that section, and shatter the very foundations of unity at which Islam aimed by giving a single prophet to the whole world.

To revert to the original subject that God even now speaks to the elect, there is a clear saying of the Holy Prophet Muhammad: "Surely there were among those before you people to whom God spoke but they were not prophets; if there be such a one among my people, it is 'Umar" (B. 62:6). This shows that, though there would be no prophets after the Holy Prophet Muhammad, yet God

FOUNDATIONS OF THE NEW ORDER

will speak to the elect among the Muslims. Not only because speaking is an attribute of the Divine Being just as hearing and seeing are His attributes, but also because it is through His word that real conviction comes to the heart that God exists, and its is through the elect that a vital faith in God is restored. They are the renewers of the faith of the masses. Such elect are specially spoken of as rising at the commencement of every century:

"Surely Allah will raise up for this community (of Muslims) at the commencement of every century one who will renew their religion" (A.D. 36:1).

Such a person is called a *mujaddid*, or a *reviver*, in the terminology of Islam, and he not only revives faith in God but also removes errors which have crept up among Muslims, and sheds new light on the great religious truths of Islam in the new circumstances which the Muslim community is called upon to face. The *Mujaddid* of the fourteenth century of the Hijrah was Hazrat Mirza Ghulam Ahmad of Qadian, the founder of the Ahmadiyya Movement - the latest revivalistic movement in Islam - who appeared at the commencement of this 14th century A.H., *i.e.*, about the year 1882 C.E.

APPENDIX I

SUMMARY OF ISLAMIC TEACHINGS

ONE GOD, ONE HUMANITY

Faith in God being the foundation of Islam, three kinds of arguments are advanced relating to the existence of God:

1. Evidence is drawn from the material universe that there must be a Creator and Controller of the universe. In the Holy Qur'an, this evidence centres round the word *Rabb*, the first attribute of the Divine Being to which Revelation draws attention -- "Read in the name of thy *Rabb*" (90:1) -- and with which the Qur'an begins (1:1), being also the oftest repeated attribute in the Holy Book. *Rabb*, usually translated as Lord for the sake of brevity, *means the Fosterer of a thing in such a manner as to make it attain one condition after another until it reaches its goal of perfection.* Everything created thus bears the impress of Divine creation in the characteristic of moving on from lower to higher stages until it reaches completion. Evolution, which has proved a stumbling block to other religions, is thus made in Islam the very basis of belief in God, and serves as an argument of purpose and wisdom in creation. The oneness of law prevailing in the universe, notwithstanding the immensity of its diversity (67:3, 4), existence of the strictest control throughout Nature from the tiniest particle to the mightiest sphere (36:38; 55:5, 6), and similar other arguments run through every page of the Holy Book.

2. The second class of arguments for the existence of God relates to the human soul in which is

implanted, according to the Holy Qur'an, the consciousness of Divine existence. An appeal is again and again made to man's inner self: "Were they created for nothing?" "Are they creators of their own souls?" "Did they create the heavens and earth?" (52:35, 36). "Am I not your *Rabb*?" (7:172). God-consciousness is thus shown to be a part and parcel of human nature. Sometimes the consciousness is mentioned in terms of the unimaginable nearness of the human spirit to the Divine spirit: "We are nearer to man than his life-vein" (50:16); "We are nearer to your soul than you" (56:85). This is to show that the consciousness of the existence of God in the human soul is even clearer than the consciousness of its own existence. This consciousness undoubtedly differs in different natures according as the inner light of man is bright or dim.

This argument is further strengthened by showing that there is something more than mere consciousness of the existence of God. The spirit of God has been breathed into man (15:29), and hence it is that the soul of man yearns after God; there is in it the instinct to serve God and to turn to Him for help (1:4). Every man, even the polytheist, turns to God in affliction and distress, when the full strength of human nature asserts itself (10:12, 22; 39:8). There is, further, implanted in man faith in God, by which he is guided through darkness and difficulty (10:9); love of God, out of which selfless service is rendered to humanity (2:177; 76:8); trust in God, which is an unfailing source of strength to man in times of failure (14:12).

3. The surest and clearest evidence of the existence of God is, however, afforded by the spiritual -- the higher -- experience of humanity, by God revealing Himself to man. The evidence of wisdom and purpose in the universe only shows that there *must be* a God, and does not lead to the certain conviction that God *is*; the evidence of the inner self of man is also insufficient to lead to this certain conviction and give man access to the Divine Being; it is Divine revelation that not only establishes the

greatest reality of this life that God *is* but also casts a flood of light on the Divine attributes, and sets man on the way by walking on which he feels His existence as a reality in his own life and which enables him to hold communion with Him. It is this realisation of the Divine Being that works a change in man's life and gives him an irresistible spiritual force through which he can bring about a change even in others' lives. God's revealing Himself to man is, according to Islam, the universal experience of humanity, the experience of men in all nations, all countries and all ages. It is this universal spiritual experience of mankind that has proved a force of the first magnitude in lifting up humanity from the depths of degradation to the great heights of moral and even material advancement.

God is above all limitations, and He cannot be likened to anything known to man (42:11). While God comprehends all vision, man's vision cannot comprehend Him (6:104). He is one; duality or trinity in Divine nature, or multiplicity of gods, is unthinkable (2:163; 16:51; 4:171); nor does He hold the relation of fatherhood or sonship to anyone (112:3; 19:90-93). Submission and service are due to Him alone (16:48, 49), and to Him alone must prayer be addressed (1:4; 72:20). Blind obedience even to religious leaders and saints, which is the same as saint-worship, is condemned (9:31). God is the Creator of all (13:16), Nourisher of all unto perfection (1:1), and the Controller of all (4:85). He is a Loving and Merciful God (11:90), His mercy embracing all things (40:7); even the most extravagant should not despair of His mercy (12:87; 39:50). He is Omniscient, knowing equally what man manifests and what he hides and even that which is in the subconscious mind (20:7). He is Omnipotent (16:48-50) and Omnipresent (58:7), being nearer to man than his own self (50:16; 56:85).

God has created man with the highest capabilities and made him a ruler in the earth (2:30; 95:40). Everything has been made subservient to man, and he can conquer the forces of Nature (14:32-34; 45:12, 13). Every man has been created in a state of purity -- none is born sinful; it is by his own misdeeds that a man degrades himself (30:30; 95:5). Everyone is by birth a Muslim, whether born of Jewish or Christian parents (30:30; B. 32:79); and all those who die before the age of discretion, whether Muslims or non-Muslims, go to heaven (B. 91:48). Islam, or submission to Divine laws, is in fact the religion of Nature (3:82), and also the natural religion of man (30:30).

The basis of all religions is faith in Divine revelation, because God is known to man and the contact of human spirit is established with the Divine spirit only through revelation. Man can make all discoveries in the sphere of the finite, but it is only by revealing Himself that the Infinite God makes Himself known to man. Hence God has been revealing Himself to man through His chosen servants in every age and every country (10:47; 35:24). Revelation is granted to man in three ways, the highest form of revelation -- revelation through the Holy Spirit -- is peculiar to prophets; in its lower forms, the infusion of an idea into the mind, a dream, a vision and *ilham*, revelation is granted to others as well, to men as well as to women (42:51; 28:7; 5:111). Only mortals to whom God revealed His will were sent as reformers because none but a mortal could serve as a model for men (17:95; 21:7, 8).

All men are a single nation (2:213; 10:19; 23:52). Their division into tribes and families (48:13) and the diversity of their tongues and colours (30:22) have nothing to do with their superiority or inferiority. The most excellent people are those who pay the greatest regard to the duties which they owe to others (48:13). Allah is the Lord of all nations (1:1). He has given all, not only what they need for their physical sustenance but also what is needed for their spiritual advancement, and hence it is that He raised prophets or warners among all nations: "There is not a people but a warner has gone among them" (35:24); "Every nation had a messenger" (10:47); "Every nation had a guide" (13:7); "We raised in every nation a messenger" (16:36); "To every nation We appointed acts of devotion" (22:67); "For every one of you We appointed a Law and a way" (5:48). The Holy Qur'an mentions by name prophets that find no mention in the Bible (7:65, 73); it also speaks of an Ethiopian prophet (31:13); of another who lived at the two Niles (18:60); and generally it says that there were prophets who have not been mentioned by name (4:164; 40:78). A Muslim is one who believes in the prophets of all the nations: "We believe in Allah and in that which has been revealed to us ..... and in that what was given to the prophets from their Lord" (2:136); "We do not make any distinction between any of His messengers" (2:285).

But a prophet to every nation was only the primary stage; the universality of revelation found further development in the idea of the World-Prophet, a single prophet for all the nations of the world: "O people! I am the Messenger of Allah to you all" (7:158); "A warner to all the nations" (25:1); "We have not sent thee but as a mercy for all the nations" (21:107); "It is naught but a reminder to all the nations" (68:52). The World-Prophet took the place of the national prophets, and the grand idea of unifying the whole human race was the grand object which revelation now aimed at. The humanitarian aspect of revelation thus does not consist only in making selfless service of humanity the object of life -- "To give away wealth out of love for Him to the near of kin and the orphans and the needy and the wayfarer and the beggars and for emancipation of slaves" (2:177); it reaches perfection in bringing about, what cannot be done by any other means, the unification of humanity.

Islam thus aims at raising the human race to the highest level to which it can rise, and it is for this reason that it claims to be a perfect religion -- "This day have I perfected for you your religion and completed on you My blessing" (5:3). It sheds complete light on all essentials of religion, on the existence and attributes of the Divine being, on the nature of Divine revelation, on the requital of good and evil, on life after death, hence its claim to be the final religion of the world. But discontinuation of prophethood is not to be confused with discontinuation of revelation. Granting of revelation to those who are not prophets being an admitted fact, the door of revelation stands open for all time, though prophethood having reached perfection has come to an end. The Holy Qur'an speaks of it as *bushra (good news)* (10:63, 64), Hadith giving it the name of *mubashshirat (good visions)* (B. 91:5). In one hadith, it is called a part of prophethood (B. 91:4); in another, the continuance of revelation is spoken of in the clearest words: "There were among those who were before you persons who were spoken to by God, though they were not prophets; if there is such a one among my people, it is "Umar" (B. 62:6). A man thus spoken to by God is called a *muhaddath* in the terminology of Islam. A *Mujaddid* is a reformer raised up by God to remove errors and shed new light on the great religious truths, and it is stated that one such person shall appear among Muslims in every century (AD. 36:1).

Religion does not consist in hard religious exercises but in living a good life, in which due regard is paid to others' rights (B. 2:29; 30:51). Good actions spring from a good heart, and hence the need of faith which rules the heart (B. 2:38). The man who has faith in God does not spare the doing of good even to a passerby, "to keep the way clear of harmful things" being a part of faith (M. 1:58). There is no faith in a man who does not "love for his brother what he loves for himself" (B. 2:6). To be a Muslim one must live a life of perfect peace with others, not causing any injury to any man, "either with his tongue or with his hand" (B. 2:3). Causing injury to another even with one's tongue is called an act of unbelief (B. 2:21).

II

THE ECONOMIC PROBLEM

Islam has not only laid down sure foundations of a peaceful World Order by creating a vital faith in God, thus deepening the roots of God-consciousness in human heart, and by bringing about a reconciliation among the irreconcilable elements of humanity, thus welding together diverse races and nations into one human race and one human nation; it has also worked out the essential details of that order, and furnished the guiding principles of a healthy social system and a sound political organisation, these being the two chief needs of a stable and lasting human civilisation.

In the social order, the economic problem occupies the first place as being the most burning question, a question which agitates every mind. The material civilisation of the West has brought about, on the one hand, a state of chaos in the international relations of humanity, and, on the other, a class-war within every nation. Whatever the basic defects, we find the socio-economic system of the Western world to have gone to two extremes, owing to its inability to meet the requirements of the new conditions. It has taken the form of either the war of capital on labour -- the war of bourgeois upon proletariat, or the war of labour on capital -- the proletariat arrayed against bourgeois. This unending war may be seen going on in every European country when the war of destruction by sword comes to an end and apparently the world is at peace. As a matter of fact, the war current disappears on the surface and takes the form of an undercurrent in national life. The sword is undoubtedly sheathed, but there is little difference so far as tyranny and injustice of man against man are concerned in this class-war and the international war of destruction.

The war in the social domain has divided the West into two camps. While in most Western countries capitalism has the upper hand and labour is the victim of tyranny, Russia has gone to the other extreme, and there the proletariat is wreaking vengeance on bourgeois with unmitigated fury. The matter does not, however, end there; the victory of labour in one country has raised hopes of similar victories in other countries, and from a war within one nation it is now assuming proportions of a world war, the Soviets being arrayed in this fight against the rest of Europe. It is true that the exigencies of the Great World War now going on have compelled new unions and Russia is to-day the ally of England and America, but in the class-war that is bound to follow the establishment of peace, the present allies will again find themselves in opposite camps.

Real alliance between England and America, on the one hand, and Russia, on the other, which is supposed to be the new foundation of peace in the world, cannot be brought about unless a reconciliation is effected between the economic ideals of these countries. So long as the economic question is not settled, there can be no real peace; and while sitting at the peace table, these powers would be preparing for another war. If this war is not to go on for ever, means and ways must be found to effect a reconciliation between these two warring classes spread over the whole world. Neither Christianity as a religion, nor the material civilisation to which it has given birth, can effect such a reconciliation. Peace proposals in this case are again in the hands of Islam, as it is only through the social order established by Islam, occupying as it does a middle position between the conflicting interests of capital and labour, that a reconciliation can be brought about and real peace established in the world.

That Islam occupies a middle position in the European war of economic ideals is admitted by many European writers. Thus Gibb, in *Whither Islam*, says towards the end:

"Within the Western world Islam still maintains the balance between exaggerated opposites. Opposed equally to the anarchy of European nationalism and the regimentation of Russian communism, it has not yet succumbed to that obsession with the economic side of life which is characteristic of present-day Europe and present-day Russia alike."

And then, quoting Professor Massingnon:

"Islam has the merit of standing for a very equalitarian conception of the contribution of each citizen by the tithe to the resources of the community; it is hostile to unrestricted exchange, to banking capital, to State loans, to indirect taxes on objects of prime necessity; but it holds to the rights of the father and the husband, to private property and to commercial capital. Here again it occupies intermediate position between the doctrines of bourgeois capitalism and Bolshevist communism" (pp. 178-79).

Islam, therefore, occupies the position of a peace-maker between the warring economic factions of different nations of the West. Its social order has several characteristics not to be met with elsewhere. In the first place, Islam does not allow the economic phase of life to so engross man's mind as to make him forgetful of the higher values of life, as the Muslims' first lesson is that duty to God takes precedence over all other duties. Whatever work he may be doing, he must give it up when he receives the call to bow before his Maker, and this call is given not only in the early morning or when one is going to bed but also in the midst of the rush of man's daily work. In obeying this call, the Muslim certainly feels the reality of the Divine presence. He knows that to earn his living he must devote his whole attention to his work, but he knows at the same time that man does not live by bread alone, and that life has a higher value to which the economic value must be subjected. Unless this truth is realised, economic competition between individuals and nations will ultimately bring woe and destruction instead of happiness of the mind. The civilised nations in their race for economic advantages have just forgotten this lesson, and hence they are working for the ruin of each other.

Secondly, the social order of Islam is an expression of Divine will, and has, therefore, a stability which man-made systems can never enjoy. Every social system of the world stands in need of a temporal power for its enforcement, but the social system of Islam works independently of rulers and governments. Communism does not exist in Russia because of its appeal to the public mind but because of its compulsory enforcement by the Soviet. Fascism too exists so long as there is a temporal power at its back. Capitalism in Europe generally retains its hold because of its great financial resources and the so-called democratic governments at its back. Real power there does not rest in the hands of the people generally but in those of the great capitalists, be they Jews or non-Jews. Not so the social order of Islam which being based on religion is an appeal to the mind, not an appeal to the arms or political power. Muslims all over the world, whether occupying the position of the rulers or the ruled, are governed by the same social laws. This is due to the fact that the social system of Islam has taken root in the minds of the people. It does not stand in need of a temporal power to enforce it.

Thirdly, the social order of Islam is the only order which has proved itself to be a World Order through the thirteen centuries of its existence. Not only are the social ideals of the numerous Muslim nations, from the far East to the farthest West, with all their racial, colour and linguistic differences, the same all over the world, but the more marvellous is the fact that while numerous changes have taken place in the social ideals of other nations during the past one thousand years, the social order of Islam has remained unchanged with all the changes in the fortunes of the Muslim nations of the world. This shows only too well that the social order of Islam has in it an inherent power which makes it indifferent to all changes and vicissitudes of fortune of the nations comprising it. It is not only a World Order; *it is the only stable World Order.*

The fourth peculiarity of the social system of Islam is that it aims at attaining equality, so far as equality is possible, for all members of a community by raising the low to the level of the high and enriching the poor. In this respect, it stands in marked contrast with Bolshevism which seeks to equalise by impoverishing the rich and bringing the high to the level of the low. A cursory glance at the Qur'anic revelations of the early period of the Holy Prophet's mission makes it clear. Islam came not only to deliver the oppressed and help the poor but to raise the poor to a higher level where they could breathe as the equals of possessors of wealth.

To attain this end, it first impressed on the minds of the rich and the poor alike that possession of heaps of gold and silver did not raise the dignity of a man, nor did poverty degrade him. Such turns of fortune did not count as anything with God, and should not count with those who believe in Him. Here are a few quotations:

"As for man, when his Lord tries him, then gives him honour and favours him, he says, My Lord honours me. But when He tries him, then straitens to him his subsistence, he says: My Lord has disgraced me" (89:15-16).

"And were it not that all people would become one (disbelieving) community, We would provide for those who disbelieve in the Beneficent, roofs of silver for their houses and stairs (of silver) by which they ascend, and (of silver) the doors of their houses and the couches on which they recline, and of gold. And all this is naught but a provision of this world's life; and the Hereafter is with thy Lord only for the dutiful" (43:33-35).

The first thing which Islam does in introducing a new social order is, therefore, to place the possession of wealth before the human mind in its true perspective. It is not a thing to be discarded. It is God Who grants the good in this life (2:201). Nor has He prohibited to any "the embellishment which He has brought forth for His servants and the good provisions" (7:32). Wealth is expressly stated to be "a means of support," and it must be placed in the hands of "the weak of understanding," who should be maintained out of its profits (4:5). But at the same time there is a warning that it is only a means to an end, *not the end*. There are higher values of life than wealth, and these must not be lost sight of in the pursuit of wealth. "The mercy of thy Lord is better than what they amass" (43:32). The highest place in human heart should, therefore, not be given to wealth, it must be reserved for God.

In the Divine scheme of social order revealed to man there is another very important consideration. There is variety throughout Nature; there are differences notwithstanding uniformity. No two men are alike; nor are their brains alike. There are differences also in the human capacity to work; nor have all equal occasions to work. Some have got better brains than others; others have a greater capacity for work; still others are placed in better environment in which their work bears better fruit. These differences cannot be obliterated. They must be accepted as one of the conditions of life:
"We apportion out among them their livelihood in the life of this world, and We exalt some of them above others in rank, that some of them may take others in service" (43:32).
"And Allah has made some of you excel others in the mean of subsistence" (16:71).

There are no means to obliterate these differences. Even Bolshevik Russia has not been able to do away with them. Stalin and a lowly peasant or a worker in the mines are not alike. This world cannot go on if some men are not held in subjection by others. If there were no differences, there would be no State, no organisation, and the whole thing would be a chaos. Differences in brain and differences in the capacity of work are recognised even in the socialist order which starts with the supposition that there must be perfect equality. The State may bring about an equal distribution of wealth by depriving the wealthy of their riches and tyrannising over them, as some States tyrannise over the poor, but this is not a solution.

The social order of Islam aims at a just and proper distribution of wealth. It introduced a unique system of doing this. To destroy capitalism -- in other words, to take away forcibly the wealth of the rich and to make it the property of the State, nominally that of the community -- would have been an act of the greatest injustice, and it was quite foreign to the spirit of Islam. It introduced a compulsory system of charity; compulsory not in the sense that any force was employed in its collection. The compulsion was moral. The individual's mentality was changed. What a man earned was the fruit of his labour, and this he could not be denied. But when he had spent what he needed out of this and saved a certain amount, this saving was treated as his capital and a fixed portion of it was to be made over to the State for the benefit of his less fortunate brethren. That share was such that it benefited the poor without impoverishing the rich. It was a Divine ordinance and man must bow before the will of God.

The amassing of wealth was regarded as carrying a certain degree of uncleanness with it, because it affected the heart of man with the love of wealth; but the uncleanness could be washed off by giving away every year one-fortieth of it for the benefit of the poor. Hence it was called *Zakat*, an act of purification. If there were a

Muslim State, it had the right to collect this due from a man's savings to be distributed among those who needed help. If there were no Muslim State, the Muslim community was still to be so organised as to be able to collect the *Zakat* to distribute it among the poor. Man's own conviction that the amassing of wealth was an impure act, and that purification could only be effected by paying two and a half per cent out of it, played -- and to this day plays -- a great part in the payment of this tax. This was only one way how Islam effected distribution of accumulated wealth. Such an attempt has not been made by any other system existing in the world.

The problem of the distribution of wealth, with which is also bound the question of political power, is undoubtedly one of the greatest problems facing humanity. The system of capitalism which is the foundation-stone, so to say, of the material civilisation of the West, has led to the concentration of wealth in fewer and fewer hands and to the growing impoverishment of the masses. Political power has followed in the wake of wealth, and at the bidding of the capitalist the politician has to declare peace and war. The insatiable thirst on the part of the capitalists, who are the real controllers of political power, has reduced many nations of the world to a state of slavery, and regular plunder has been legalised under different high-sounding phrases such as colonisation, occupation, mandate, sphere of influence and so on. The great powers are only great capitalists on a national scale; at the same time they help capitalism by their huge borrowings to wage war against other nations. Islam remedies this evil by prohibiting usury, which will, however, be dealt with further on.

The reaction against capitalism set in towards the middle of the nineteenth century, almost a hundred years ago. It came under the name of socialism, and gradually developed into what is known as Bolshevism. It holds Russia in its grip, perhaps as severely as capitalism still holds other European countries. Outside Russia it has made very little headway, though a very strong propaganda has been carried on by Russia. Whether it has come to stay in Russia itself is a question which only the future can decide. But there is one thing that strikes one as very strange. Bolshevism, which had come to liberate the people, is as much of a bondage as capitalism. The autocracy of Czardom has only given place to the autocracy of the Soviet.

The question before us, however, is: Has Bolshevism, by State-ownership of industry, finally solved the great problem of the distribution of wealth? To say that because the Five-Year Plan in Russia has accelerated production to an extent which could hardly be imagined, and that therefore the State-ownership of industry is the solution of the problem, is to show overhastiness in drawing a conclusion. Who knows that the people entrusted with the carrying out of the scheme, the State agents, may not to-morrow degenerate into an oligarchy similar to the oligarchy of capitalism! Human nature is too prone to such tendencies and Bolshevism hardly offers any remedy to check them. But there is more than this. Bolshevism which came as the friend of labour defeats its own end by denying to labour its fruits. The rigid system of doling out the necessaries of life to all alike, to the indolent and the hard worker, to the stupid and the intelligent, will undoubtedly foster conditions which must soon become unbearable; it is going directly against Nature and Nature's recognised laws. Its evil results cannot be seen in a day. It took centuries to make manifest the evils of capitalism, and it will take a long time to make prominent the evils of Bolshevism.

To Islam is due the credit of not only solving the wealth problems, but at the same time, developing the higher sentiments and building up a character, on which alone can be laid the foundation of a lasting civilisation for the human race. The rigid laws of Bolshevism, which care only for the body, giving it sufficient to live on, will kill the higher sentiments of sympathy and love, qualities which not only make life worth living but lacking which humanity must degenerate into the worst barbarism. Islam accomplishes both objects by *Zakat*, its State institution of charity. *Zakat* acts not only as a levelling influence, but also as a means of developing the higher sentiments of man, the sentiments of love and sympathy towards fellowmen, while the rigid system of State-ownership helps to kill man's higher instincts. By this means, too, wealth is made to circulate in the body politic of Islam, just as blood circulates in a living organism; a fixed portion of the wealth of the richer members is drawn to the centre, whence it is sent forth to those parts of the body politic which need it most. The institution of *Zakat* thus helps not only a proper distribution of wealth but also becomes a means of the uplift of the nation as a whole.

It should be borne in mind that *Zakat* is not simply an obligatory charity; it is a State institution, or, where there is no Muslim State, a national institution. The individual is not at liberty to calculate and spend the *Zakat* as he likes. It must be collected by the State or by a national organisation, and then spent on the community. The donor is not required to give a certain portion of his savings to deserving persons as charity, but to contribute the same to a fund which must be used for the uplift of the community.

State-ownership of industry and property, which is the only alternative to the *Zakat* or tithe system of the Islamic social order, is sometimes glibly talked of as being the best economic solution for this world. The first question is: Does it increase the wealth of the country? The harder a people work and the greater their intelligence in labour, the richer would they be in commanding the resources of Nature, which, in other words, is wealth. But State-ownership of industry and absence of all private enterprise precludes all competition and all incentive to hard and intelligent labour, and, in the end, it will, by promoting habits of indolence and apathy, lower the standard of productiveness and impoverish the nation which adopts it. National consciousness, the desire to live as a separate, powerful and independent nation, may for some time act as an incentive, but this too because of the presence of competition on a national scale. In times of war, this incentive may even be very great when there is fear of being destroyed by a more powerful nation, as it has been in Russia. But that the absence of private enterprise and private ownership in peaceful times will promote habits of indolence and sloth, is too patent a fact to be denied, and even the Soviet has been compelled to modify its first views and to introduce competition in some form.

State-ownership of property, however, which is only a natural corollary to State-ownership of industry, will result in worse conditions than those which capitalism has brought about. The evils of capitalism become more intense as the number of capitalists decreases. The less the number of competitors in the field, the greater the evil which capitalism brings in its train. And when there is only one capitalist in the field, be it the State or individual, the evils of capitalism would appear in the intensest form. Nay, a single individual as the sole capitalist in a nation would be more bearable in comparison with the State as the owner of all property and industry. An individual could be easily criticised, and he may have to mend his ways in his own interests; not so the State which can, and often does, stifle all criticism which it thinks to be adverse to its interest. There is a remedy in this world for every tyranny but there is no remedy for the tyranny of the State, more particularly of a State which is also the sole capitalist in a country. To say that such a capitalist State will work for the benefit of the masses is as baseless an assertion as the other one that an autocrat works only for the benefit of those who are under his sway. The State is, in fact, a necessary evil to curb the dangerous elements in society; its tyranny is now and then fearful. But it will be most fearful when it holds in its hands all the financial resources of which all others are deprived. To invest the State with the sole ownership of industry and property is, therefore, to give in its hands a most dangerous weapon of tyranny, and its devastations would be much more terrific than the devastations of the world wars with which humanity is faced to-day.

The social order of Islam does not interfere with private ownership of industry and property, does not deprive a man of the fruits of his labour, and leaves an open field for competition, for hard work and for the exercise of intelligence. But it tries to bring about a just distribution of wealth by requiring the capitalists, the possessors of wealth, to give away a part of their wealth for the benefit of the less favoured members of society. It also works to increase the number of capitalists so that competition, being widened as much as possible, may be healthier. The *Zakat* is in fact meant to enable the poorer members of the community to start business with a small capital and then to increase it by their own diligence and hard work.

In addition to *Zakat*, there is the Islamic law of inheritance by which wealth is sought to be distributed among larger numbers, and the number of small capitalists is thus increased. Even after paying the *Zakat*, one-fortieth of his accumulated wealth every year, a man leaves some wealth at his death, as every diligent and hard worker must. This wealth, according to the Islamic social order, does not become the property of one person, as in the generally prevailing law of primogeniture. Islam introduced a twofold reform into the existing laws of inheritance; it made the female a co-sharer with the male, and it ordered the division of property among all the heirs on a democratic basis. One big capitalist is thus replaced on his death by many small capitalists. The general law is thus laid down in the Holy Qur'an: "Men shall have a portion of what the parents and the near relatives leave, and women shall have a portion of what the parents and the near relatives leave, whether there is little of it or much" (4:7).

Before the advent of Islam, the Arabs had a very strong and, to all appearance, a very sound, tradition that he alone should inherit who could smite with the spear, and therefore no portion of the inheritance was given to such of the heirs as were not capable of meeting the enemy and fighting in battles. This tradition strongly appealed to a people among whom tribal fighting was carried on day and night. Woman, as in the Jewish law, was looked upon as a part of the property of the deceased, to say nothing of her inheriting the property. And just when a defensive war against the whole of Arabia was being carried on by a handful of Muslims, the prevailing law of inheritance was declared to be unjust, and a new law given which put widows and orphans on a level of equality with those who fought for the defence of the tribe and the country. So great was the faith of Muslims in God that the new order was accepted without demur.

The new order divided heirs into two groups, the first group consisting of children, parents, and husband or wife, and the second consisting of brothers and sisters. All the persons mentioned in the first group are immediate sharers, and if all of them are living they have all of them a right in the property. The members of the second group only inherit if all or some of the members of the first group are wanting. Both groups are capable of further extension, grandchildren, or still lower descendants, taking the place of children, grandparents or still higher ascendants taking the place of parents, and uncles, aunts and other distant relatives taking the place of brothers and sisters.

There is yet a third phase of the Islamic social order which regulates a just distribution of wealth. It is the relation between the debtor and the lender. Whereas the debtor is required to be very faithful in repaying the debt -- "Among the best of you are those who are good in payment of debt," according to a saying of the Holy Prophet -- the lender is required to be very lenient, to have more regard for his fellowman than for his money. The basic outlook of

THE ECONOMIC PROBLEM

Islam on human society is that one in distress must be helped. It is laid down in the Holy Qur'an: "If (the debtor) is in straitness, let there be postponement till (he is in) ease. And that you remit (it) as alms is better for you, if you only knew" (2:280). This principle was worked out most liberally by the Holy Prophet as the head of the Muslim State which came into existence towards the end of his life. "I am nearer to the believers," he said, "than themselves; so whoever of the believers dies and leaves a debt, its payment is on me; and whoever leaves property, it is for his heirs" (B. 69:5). A debt contracted for a right cause was thus to be paid by the State if the debtor could not pay it.

It is for this reason too that the social order of Islam does not allow usury. The prohibition of usury is clearly associated in the Holy Qur'an with charity, for inasmuch as charity is the broad basis of human sympathy, usury annihilates all sympathetic affection. The usurer is likened to one whom the devil has prostrated by his touch so that he is unable to arise. Such is, in fact, the usurer who would not hesitate to reduce the debtor to the last straits if thereby he might add a penny to his millions. He grows in selfishness until he is divested of all sympathetic feelings, and greed rules his heart. Islam is basically opposed to this.

Usury, moreover, promotes habits of idleness, since the usurer, instead of doing any hard work or manual labour, becomes like the parasite, living on the labour of others. In the great struggle that is going on between capital and labour, Islam sides with labour, and, by its prohibition of usury, tries to restore the balance between the two, not allowing capital to enthral labour. It is in reference to the honourable place that Islam gives to labour that the Holy Qur'an says that "Allah has allowed trade and forbidden usury", for while trading requires the use of labour and skill and elevates the morals, usury promotes habits of indolence, cunning and oppression. To help the distressed one who is in straits is the object of the social structure of Islam, and to reduce him to further straits is the end of usury; hence usury is called "war with Allah and His Messenger" (2:279).

The prohibition is not limited to what may technically be called *usury*. It includes all kinds of interest, whether the rate be high or low, and whether the interest is or is not added to the principal after fixed periods. Indeed, all interest has a tendency to assume, ultimately, the form of usury, and becomes oppressive for the debtor, a fact which is borne out by the history of indebtedness in all countries. It is sometimes argued that the prohibition of interest would be a serious drawback in the carrying on of trade and business transactions and also in the execution of important national schemes. Even if this be a drawback, it would be more than compensated by making impossible the world wars which entail untold misery on the human race and which are due simply to usurious borrowings. But let us look at facts. Trade was actually carried on, on the vastest scale, and important national schemes were carried into effect, by the great Muslim nations of early days spread over vast territories, they being the vanguards of the great nations of the world in the march of civilisation. True it is that the prohibition does not fit in with the modern world conditions which have been brought about by the material civilisation of the West, but the high ideal which Islam sets before itself is not unworkable, and did practically work for centuries in early Islamic civilisation.

Interest on the capital with which a business is run differs a little from interest on ordinary debts. It is, in fact, a case in which capital and labour are sharers. Such a partnership is not disallowed, but the social order of Islam requires that both capital and labour should be sharers in profit as well as in loss. The payment of interest at a fixed rate means that capital shall always have a profit even though the business may be running at a loss. It is sometimes urged that to make capital and labour share in profit as well as in loss is impracticable because it requires the keeping of an account. But the keeping of account is really a necessity of trade. Moreover, accounts have to be kept for purposes of taxation; they are also kept by all joint stock companies which carry on trade on the largest scale. This method is more advatageous for the general welfare of the community than the method of charging interest on capital, which increases the evils of capitalism and is unjust to labour. Borrowings by a State or a company for the purpose of executing big projects, such as the building of railways and canals, etc., may follow the same principle; and the banking system generally, if moulded on a co-operative basis, such as the social system of Islam requires, would be a blessing for humanity.

There are some other arrangements too for minimising the evils of capitalism in the Islamic social order, but I would mention only one more. It is the injunction relating to bequests. According to the Holy Qur'an, everyone who leaves wealth after him is required to bequeath a certain amount of it -- not more than one-third, according to a saying of the Holy Prophet -- for charitable objects, among which the help of the poor, the widows and the orphans occupies a high place. This, according to the Holy Qur'an, is obligatory:
"It is prescribed for you, when death approaches one of you, if he leaves behind wealth for parents and near relatives, to make a bequest in a kindly manner; it is incumbent upon the dutiful" (2:180).

The bequest, according to a saying of the Holy Prophet, was meant for charitable objects, and was not to exceed one-third of the property of a person, so that the heirs may not be left destitute. The bequest would be as profitable a source for the amelioration of the poor as the *Zakat*, and if the State makes it obligatory, it would be quite in consonance with the letter and spirit of the Holy Qur'an.

APPENDIX

SUMMARY OF ISLAMIC TEACHINGS

Economic Aspect

In the Islamic social order, the highest place of honour is given to labour. "No one eats better food than that which he eats out of the work of his hand," the Holy Prophet is reported to have said (B. 34:15). And he added: "The Prophet of God, David, ate out of the work of his hand." Even the tending of goats for remuneration is considered honourable, the Holy Prophet himself doing this work "for some carats" in his earlier days (B. 7:2). His companions did not disdain the work of a porter (B. 24:10), and they were advised to earn their livelihood, if necessary, by bringing "a bundle of firewood" on their backs and selling it in the market (B. 24:50). The humblest work carried with it a dignity; those who followed the profession of a butcher or a seller of meat, a goldsmith, a blacksmith, a tailor, a weaver or a carpenter were looked upon as honourable members of the society (B. 34:21, 28-32). The Holy Prophet himself did the work of mending his clothes and his shoes, milking his goats, cleansing his utensils with his own hands; and though he occupied the high dignity of a spiritual teacher and a king at one and the same time, yet within his house, he helped his wife in her house-hold work (B. 10:44). Women, too, did work of labour like men.

Withholding the remuneration of a labourer is denounced in the strongest terms: "On the Day of Resurrection I shall be the adversary in dispute of a person ..... who employs a servant and receives fully the labour due from him, then does not pay his remuneration"

(B. 34:106). On the other hand, it is an act of great virtue to invest the unpaid remuneration of a labourer in a profitable business, so that it should become abundant wealth (B. 37:12). The basic rule is laid down in the Holy Qur'an that the servant shall do his work faithfully and to the best of his ability, and that the master shall pay him fully for the service rendered (B. 28:25, 26). The servant must be treated on a perfect basis of equality in all other matters, so much so that he may dine on the same table with his master (B.42:18). The master and the servant are, in fact, considered to be two contracting parties, and the one is not considered to be higher in status than the other, simply on account of this relation (B. 37:14).

The outlook of Islam on wealth is quite different from that of the modern civilisation which considers it as the be-all and the end-all of life. Economic gains have a secondary place in Islam, duty to God taking precedence of all other duties. "People used to buy and sell and carry on trade," we are told in a hadith, "but when it was the turn of a duty out of the duties imposed by Allah, neither merchandise nor selling diverted them from the remembrance of Allah" (B. 34:8). The Holy Qur'an speaks of the activities of Muslims in similar words (24:37). Islam gives wealth its rightful place as the means to an end: "Your wealth, God has made if for you a means of support" and it is therefore not to be wasted by handing it over to the weak of understanding (4:5); it should not be squandered wastefully (17:26) or spent extravagantly (25:67). But possession of wealth does not necessarily carry honour with it, nor does any disgrace attach to being in straitened circumstances (89:15, 16). The amassing of wealth, on the other hand, takes away contentment of mind and ends in disaster (104:2-4).

Again, wealth is considered to be the fruit of labour, and everyone, man or woman, has a right to earn wealth by his or her labour: "Men shall have the benefit of what they earn and women shall have the benefit of what they earn"

(4:32). In fact, to deny possession of wealth to anyone earning it is to deny the fruit of labour. Wealth may also be inherited by both men and women (4:7). It may also be given or taken as a gift (4:4; B. 51:1). There is no limit to the wealth which a man may possess (4:20); but everyone who possesses about Rs. 50 or more is required to pay *Zakat*, *i.e.* two and a half per cent of his savings annually, which goes to a common fund for the help of the poor (9:60; B. 24:1, 4; Msh. 6:1). This fund is to be managed by the Muslim State or the Muslim community. *Zakat* is not charity in the true sense of the word; it is a tax payable to the State or an organised body; only one-third may be left, if necessary, with the individual, for distribution according to his choice (Msh. 6:1).

The conception of charity is very broad in Islam, including the doing of any good to a fellow-man, or helping him in any matter, or refraining from doing him evil, or showing him the right way or meeting him with a cheerful countenance, and so on (B. 24:31; 56:72). Doing good to dumb animals is also charity (Msh. 6:6). Charity must be given and should not be asked; the humblest work is recommended as being more honourable than begging (B. 24:50). It may be given openly as in the case of a contribution to public charitable funds, or in secret (2:271).

Among means of livelihood, trade occupies the most prominent place; the honest merchant is ranked with the righteous servants of God who devote their lives to the service of humanity (Tr. 12:4). The seller is required to be just in weighing or measuring (17:35), generous in dealing (B. 34:16), giving respite even to those in easy circumstances and forgiving those in straitened circumstances (B. 34:16). If there is a defect in the thing sold, it must be made manifest to the purchaser (B. 34:19). The buyer should be given the opportunity to examine the thing purchased (B. 34:62). Special directions are given as to the sale of cereals, as they are the prime need of every man. They should be sold in the market so that they may be had at the price which the producer obtained (B. 34:49). Speculation in cereals is prohibited (B. 34:54). The withholding of cereals to raise their price artificially is forbidden (Msh. 12:8). Immoveable property, it is recommended, should only be sold if the seller intends investing the price in other immoveable property (Ah. IV:307).

Cultivation of land and planting of fruit trees is spoken of as an act of great merit (B. 41:1); but the warning is given at the same time that a people who give themselves up entirely to agriculture neglecting other lines of their development cannot rise to eminence (B. 41:2). Impetus is given to the cultivation of waste-land by giving a preferential right to such cultivators (B. 41:15). Private ownership of land is recognised and the owner of land has a right to let it for cultivation to another person (B. 41:19); but it is recommended that those who possess vast tracts of land and can afford should allow their lands to be cultivated rent-free by their poorer brethren (Msh. 12:13). The State's claim on produce of land is limited to one-tenth in the case of land watered by rain or by natural channels running on the surface, and to one-twentieth in the case of land watered by wells (B. 24:55). A man encroaching on his neighbour's land is threatened with the severest punishment (B. 46:14).

All transactions relating to borrowing and lending must be put to writing and the interest of the debtor must be specially guarded (2:282). A man must avoid contracting debts as far as possible (B. 39:3; 43:10). Contracting a debt when one does not intend to pay it is denounced (B. 43:2). Granting respite to a debtor and the remission of debt when the debtor is in straitened circumstances are laudable acts (B. 34:17). It is good to make payment in excess of the sum which a person owes (B. 43:7). Deferring payment of debt by one who has the means is not only unjust, it may even be punished (B. 43: 13). Mortgaging of property as security for payment is allowed subject to certain conditions (2:283; B. 43:1; 48:9). Usury is prohibited (2:275).

Everyone possessing wealth is required to make a will for charitable objects to the extent of one-third of his property (2:180; B. 55:1; 23:37). What remains of the property of a deceased person after payment of debts and execution of the will should be divided among the relatives, both male and female (4:11, 12). If there are no near or distant relatives to inherit, the property of a deceased Muslim would vest in the Muslim State, or when there is no Muslim State, in the Muslim community.

III

THE HOME

A right solution of the sex problem is as essential for a well-built social order as that of the economic question. The home is the unit of human society. The sum total of human happiness under ordinary circumstances is determined by the happiness which prevails in the home, and the stability of the home is an index of the stability of society and of its civilisation. As the male and the female together make a home, it is on a right understanding of their position and relations that the happiness and stability of the home depends.

Humanity has taken a very long time to understand the true position of woman. For long ages she was looked upon as a slave, as the property of her husband, not as his equal. A person was one who could own property but a woman could not own any property or carry on any transaction in her own name, and she was not therefore a person in the real sense of the word. She had very few rights as a daughter, as a wife, even as a mother. As a daughter she was the property of her father; as a wife, that of her husband. Half the human race -- the very half that was responsible for bringing up the human race -- was relegated to the position of slavery. If woman was thus deprived even of the material benefits of life, how could she be deemed fit to receive spiritual benefits? Marriage itself was considered to be a hindrance in the spiritual progress of man even by Christianity.

With the slackening of the hold of Christianity, and the advancement of material civilisation, woman started a fight for her rights, and in this she has been successful to some extent. But along with this gain in the temporal field, there has been a set-back so far as the happiness and stability of home-life are concerned. Materialism weakened the controlling force of religion and led to loose ideas about the relationship between the sexes. The result is that Europe is leaning more and more to "free love," and marriage is discarded, not on account of any inherent defect in it, but because it entails certain responsibilities on the two partners who are required to build up the home. The materialistic outlook on life makes a man selfish, and while he runs after every enjoyment, he shirks the serious responsibilities of life, so that he may be able to lead a carefree life. But life has its cares and sorrows as well as its pleasures, and marriage, while strengthening the ties of the mutual love between the male and the female, thereby increasing their happiness, requires them to share each other's cares and sorrows as well. "Free love" makes each of the mates selfish in the extreme, because while the male and the female become each other's partners in pleasure, each is free to leave the other uncared for in his or her sorrow.

The social system of Islam brought about a revolution in stabilising the relations between the two sexes. It started with the strengthening of the foundations by recognising woman as a free person who had the legal right to own property and to dispose it of as she liked. In this regard, she was the equal of man in all respects. She was no more the property of the male but his partner and his equal having the same rights to earn and own property as the male. The foundation was thus laid of removing the bondage of half the human race. From being a property woman became a person whose status was not in any way inferior to that of man. She could earn money; she could do any work which she liked and she was entitled to the fruit of her labour just as man was. This revolution regarding the position of woman was brought about thirteen hundred years ago in the following words:

"Men shall have the benefit of what they earn and women shall have the benefit of what they earn" (4:32).

Woman could thus earn and own property just as man could. The social system of Islam recognised no difference between the two sexes in this respect. She could buy or sell as a man could; she could even give it as a free gift to anyone she liked:
"But if they (the women) of themselves be pleased to give to you a portion thereof, consume it with enjoyment and pleasure" (4:4).

Islam, however, did not stop at this reform which was in itself a marvel. It also made woman inherit property just like the male. The Arabs had a very strong tradition that only he could inherit who was able to defend the tribe against the onslaughts of an enemy, a work for which nature had not designed woman. The principle, however, with which Islam started equality of the status of woman with that of man was worked out in all details of life. If she could earn and own property, if she could dispose it of as she liked, she could not be deprived of inheriting property, and the general rule is thus laid down:
"For man is a share of what the parents and the near relatives leave, and for women a share of what the parents and the near relatives leave" (4:7).

Such was the change brought about by the social system of Islam in the temporal position of woman. The same principle was applied in the spiritual domain; woman was on a par with man spiritually too:
"I (God) will not suffer the work of any worker among you to be lost whether male or female, the one of you being from the other (3:194).
"And whoever does good, whether male or female, and he (or she) is a believer, these shall enter the Garden" (40:40).

"Whoever does good, whether male or female, and he (or she) is a believer, We shall certainly give them their reward for the best of what they did" (16:97).

The Holy Qur'an speaks of women even receiving Divine revelation, God's greatest gift to man (3:41; 28:7). Hence marriage, according to Islam, is not a hindrance in the spiritual progress of man; it is rather a help, a means leading to the development of the spiritual faculties of man. God created mates that they may find "quiet of mind" in each other (30:21); "The women are an apparel for you and you are an apparel for them" (2:187).

Mutual love between husband and wife -- a love based not on momentary passion but on a life-long connection -- and the consequent parental love for the offspring -- leads to a very high development of the feeling of love of man for man as such, and this in its turn leads to the disinterested service of humanity. The natural inclination of the male to the female and of the female to the male finds expression through marriage, and is developed, first, into a love for the children, then into a love for one's kith and kin, and ultimately into a disinterested love for the whole of humanity. The home is in fact the first training ground of love and service. Here a man finds real pleasure in suffering for the sake of others, and the sense of service is then gradually developed and broadened.

Marriage is thus regarded by Islam as a means to the moral uplift of man, a means for the development of those feelings of love and service which are the pride of humanity to-day. Hence, according to the social code of Islam, marriage is the normal condition in which every man and woman ought to live. The Holy Qur'an enjoins upon all its followers to live in a married state: "And marry those among you who are single" (24:32). The Holy Prophet is reported to have said to certain young men, on noticing monkish inclinations in them: "I am married;

whoever inclines to any way other than my way, is not of me" (B. 67:1). And on another occasion: "O assembly of young people! whoever of you has the means to support a wife, he should get married, for this is the best means of keeping the looks cast down and guarding chastity" (B. 67:2). According to another of his sayings, "The man who marries perfects half his religion."

According to the Islamic social system, marriage is a contract (4:21), and it is entered into by mutual consent expressed by the two parties, the man and the woman, in the presence of witnesses. This again shows that the male and the female in the Islamic home are two partners standing on the same level and having both their rights and obligations. Being, however, the basis on which human society is built, the marriage contract is not like an ordinary contract. It is necessary that publicity should be given to it. The one fact that distinguishes marriage from fornication is its publicity (4:24; 5:5). Every contract of marriage must be made publicly known, even with the beat of drums, and it must be made in a public place: "Make public this marriage and perform it in the mosques and beat drums for it" (Msh. 13:4).

In addition to its publicity, the marriage contract is given a sacred character by the delivery of a sermon, before the announcement of marriage is made. In the sermon, certain verses of the Holy Qur'an (3:111; 4:1; 33:70, 71) are recited. These verses call attention to the one great need of life, its central fact; that there is a God above to Whom both the male and the female are responsible. The contract, therefore, must not be taken lightly. Every right which the parties have, and every obligation which they owe to each other, is a duty imposed by God, Whose Law is the greatest of all the laws. A dowry is also settled on the woman at the time of the marriage. The settling of a dowry which amounts to making her owner of some property shows that on accepting her position as wife, the woman, instead of losing any of her rights as an individual, acquires a full and independent status as a person.

The individuality of the wife is not merged into that of her husband in the social system of Islam. While she loses none of her rights which she possesses as an individual member of society, her new life brings with it new responsibilities which carry with them new rights: "They (the wives) have rights similar to their obligations in a just manner" (2:228). The broad rule is laid down in the Hadith: "Everyone of you is a ruler and everyone shall be questioned about those entrusted to his care; the king is a ruler, and the man is a ruler over the people of his house, and the woman is a ruler over the house of her husband and his children" (B. 67:91). The home is a unit in the greater organization of a nation, and just as in the vaster national organisation, there must be somebody to exercise the final authority, the smaller organisation of the home needs a similar arrangement. The husband is first spoken of as being "a ruler over the people of his house," and the wife is then described as "a ruler over the house of her husband and his children." The home is thus a State in miniature, where authority is exercised by both the husband and the wife. But unless one of them is given a higher authority, there would be chaos in this kingdom. The reason for giving the higher authority to the husband is thus stated in the Holy Qur'an: "Men are the maintainers of women because Allah has made some of them to excel others and because they spend out of their property" (4:34). The husband provides maintenance for the wife and has the final charge of the affairs of the home, thus exercising authority over the wife when there is need for it. It is the man who can be entrusted with the maintenance of the family, and therefore it is he who must hold the higher authority.

The functions of the husband and the wife are quite distinct, and each is entrusted with the functions which are best suited for his or her nature. Man excels woman in physique and constitution; he is capable of bearing greater hardships and facing greater dangers. On the other hand, woman excels man in the qualities of love and affection. Nature, for her own purpose of helping the growth of creation, has endowed the female among mankind as well as the lower animals, with the quality of love to a much higher degree than the male. Hence there is a natural division as between man and woman of the main work which is to be carried on for the good and progress of humanity. Man is suited to face the hard struggles of life on account of his stronger physique; woman is suited to bring up children because of the preponderance of the quality of love in her. The duty of the maintenance of the family has, therefore, been entrusted to man, and the duty of bringing up the children to woman. And each is vested with the authority suited to the function with which he or she is entrusted.

This division of work is only the general rule; it does not mean that woman has entirely been excluded from other kinds of activity. Notwithstanding her rightful position in the home, as the manager of the household and the upbringer of children, woman took interest in all the national activities of the Muslim community. The care of the children did not prevent her from repairing to the mosque to join the congregational prayer (B. 10:162); nor was this care an obstacle in her way to join the soldiers in the field of battle to perform a large number of duties, such as the carrying of provisions (B. 56:66), taking care of the sick and the wounded (B. 56:67), removing the wounded and the slain from the battlefield (B. 56:68), etc. She could do any work she liked. Women helped their husbands in the labour of the field (B. 67:108); they could carry on business (B. 11:40); they could sell to and purchase from men, and men could sell to and purchase from them (B. 34:67). Similarly, men would help their wives in the household work.

Great stress is laid on good and kindly treatment towards the wife in the Islamic social order. "Keep them in good fellowship," "Treat them kindly" are the oft-recurring orders (2:229, 231; 4:19). Kindness to the wife is recommended even when a man dislikes her, for "it may be that you dislike a thing while Allah has placed abundant good in it" (4:19). The Hadith lays equally great stress upon good treatment of the wife. There is a most famous saying of the Holy Prophet: "The most excellent of you is he who is best in his treatment of his wife" (Msh. 13:11). In his famous address at the Farewell Pilgrimage, he again laid stress on the good treatment of women: "O my people! you have certain rights over your wives and so have your wives over you. They are the trust of Allah in your hands. So you must treat them with all kindness" (M. 15:19).

Though marriage, according to Islam, is only a social contract, yet the rights and responsibilities consequent upon it are of such importance to the welfare of humanity that a high degree of sanctity is attached to it. But in spite of the sacredness of its character, Islam recognises the necessity, in exceptional circumstances, of keeping the way open for the dissolution of the marriage tie. Before Islam, people went generally to one or the other extreme in the matter of divorce. According to the Hindu law, marriage once performed can never be dissolved. The right of divorce, according to the Jewish law, belongs to the husband who can exercise it at his will. The Christian law recognises the right of divorce only when there is faithlessness on the part of either of the parties, but the divorced parties are precluded from marrying again. Islam adopts a middle course among all these extremes. It allows divorce but considers it a hateful thing; it requires the exploration of all possible ways of reconciliation; and, while recognising the wife's right to divorce for any sufficient reason, restricts the husband's right to it.

The principle underlying divorce, according to the Holy Qur'an, is the decision no longer to live together as husband and wife. In fact, marriage itself is an agreement to live together as husband and wife, and therefore when either of the parties finds itself unable to agree to such a life, divorce must follow. The Muslim mentality in this matter is, however, one of hatred for getting a divorce: "With Allah the most detestable of all things permitted is divorce" (AD. 13:3). When one of the couple feels that he or she cannot pull on with the other, he or she is told to bear in mind that "it may be that you dislike a thing while Allah has placed abundant good in it" (4:19). Remedies are also suggested to avoid divorce so long as possible: "And if you fear a breach between the two, appoint a judge from his people and a judge from her people; if they both desire agreement, Allah will effect harmony between them" (4:35). It is due to such teachings that the mentality of a Muslim is to face the difficulties of married life along with its comforts, and to avoid disruption of marital relations so long as possible, turning to divorce only as the last resort. Hence, in spite of the facility with which divorce may be effected, there being no need to go to the court in most cases, its incidence is much smaller among Muslims as compared with Christian countries, where the binding force of the social laws of Islam does not exist, and where therefore the percentage of divorces is very great.

Another distinguishing characteristic of the Islamic social order is that it places the highest value on chastity. To guard the chastity of women it has adopted certain measures which have been misunderstood by the critics of Islam. A cursory glance at the different societies of the world would show that so far as sexual morality is concerned, the Islamic society stands on a very high level. Prostitution which is so rampant in Western countries, and which in India is associated even with religious life, is almost unknown to Muslim countries. It prevailed in Arabia before the advent of Islam, but Islam eradicated it so thoroughly that it has not taken root anywhere in Muslim society. The prevalence of this evil is due, among other reasons, such as uncurbed sexual lust and a low moral standard in sexual matters, to the excess of women over men in most countries, a fact which census figures have now made only too clear. The number of women in almost all European countries is much in excess of men and the terrible wars which seem to have become now a part of the normal life of Europe are further increasing that number. How is that excess number of women to be dealt with, is a question for the moralists of Europe. Nature will have its course, and if no measures are adopted in time, the growing evil of prostitution, already a blot on the fair name of the womanhood of Europe, will bring down the very foundations of European society.

Islam was faced with a similar situation in its early history. The wars with the non-Muslim Arab population, which were forced on Muslims because of the determination of their opponents to destroy Islam, reduced the number of the males to a very large extent, and many homes were filled with widows and orphans. Islam foresaw the evil result in all its clearness. An arrangement could be easily made to supply the destitute with bread, but the nature made by God could not be changed, and sexual appetite was as certain a reality as physical appetite. It was under these conditions that Islam allowed a limited polygamy. The verse which permits polygamy clearly refers to these circumstances. It opens with the words: "If you fear that you cannot act equitably towards (widows and) orphans[10] marry such women as seem good to you" (4:3). Polygamy was permitted not because men wanted more wives than one, but because widows and orphans were left unprotected and it was necessary to provide homes for them. Islam aimed at the building up of

---

10. Yatama is the plural of yatim which means, in the case of children one who has lost his father, and in the case of women, one who has lost her husband. Even if the word yatama meant only children who had lost their male parents, the context shows that the widows or the mothers of the orphans are included here.

character in the first instance, and it could not be satisfied with the sympathetic materialist's solution of giving bread to woman without caring for her soul, without providing a home for her, without making arrangements for guarding her chastity, without giving her the means by which she could attain to her perfection as a woman. The materialist's solution is easy, but it is a solution relating only to her body; he would not care for her chastity or for her soul; he would not care even if she has to sell her chastity for a few shillings, sometimes even to support her body. This is not an exaggeration; this is what is actually happening in every great centre of the materialistic civilisation, where woman is sometimes forced to sell her chastity for food or for shelter.

Such a solution was repugnant to Islam. Its concern was the soul in the first instance; it placed a high value upon the chastity of woman and it had to provide a means to guard it first. So the Holy Prophet under Divine guidance allowed a limited polygamy, which prophets before him had also allowed. Other arrangements could be made for the maintenance of widows, but home-life could not be given to them in any other manner, and home-life is the real source whence spring all those good qualities of love and affection which are the greatest assets of social life and civilisation. Islam bases its civilisation on home-life, and under exceptional circumstances, where monogamy fails to provide homes to women, it allows a limited polygamy to extend to them that advantage. Even if it be half a home that a woman finds in a polygamous family, it is better than no home at all. And what does this 'no home' mean? Not only that woman has no shelter; not only that she is deprived of an occasion to develop her God-given faculties of love and affection; it also means in most cases a moral depravity which is the greatest danger to civilisation. Monogamy is undoubtedly the right rule of life under normal conditions, but when abnormal conditions are brought about by the excess of females over males, monogamy fails, and it is only through a limited polygamy that this difficulty can be solved. Europe is today confronted with that question independently of war, and war which must always be a source of decrease in the number of the males, bringing about a corresponding increase in the number of women, only aggravates its seriousness. Professions may be opened for woman to enable her to earn bread, and Islam never closed the door of any profession against woman. But the crux of the question is not the provision of bread but the provision of a home. It must be clearly understood that polygamy in Islam is, both in theory and practice, an exception, and as an exception it is a remedy for many of the evils of modern civilisation. Even if Europe considers it to be an evil: let it ponder which is the greater evil - a limited polygamy or an unlimited prostitution and moral degeneration.

In another way, too, Islam aims at raising the moral status of society and to minimise chances of illicit sexual relations growing up between the sexes, so that the home may be a haven of peace for the husband, the wife and the children. This is effected by a division of work, woman being concerned more with the management of the house and the upbringing of the children, and man with their maintenance. The division reduces to the minimum the chances of the intermingling of the two sexes. It does not mean that woman shall not go out of her house; she has full liberty to go out for her needs (B. 65:33:8).

The division of work not only improves the quality of work; it also improves the moral tone of society. Another measure to gain this end is the stress laid upon the privacy of home-life. Going into houses without permission is strictly forbidden (24:27), and may be avoided so long as the necessary work can be done without interfering with the privacy of women (33:53).

The third measure to achieve this end is that the women should be properly dressed when appearing on public occasions, or when otherwise intermingling of the sexes becomes necessary. Their proper dress is that the whole body should be covered with the exception of the face and hands (24:30, 31; AD. 31:30). They are forbidden when going out of their houses and appearing in public to make a display of their finery (33:33), or to uncover parts of the body which excite the sensual passions of the opposite sex (24 : 31). As a further precaution both sexes are required to behave modestly and to develop the habit of keeping their looks cast down in the presence of each other:

"Say to the believing men that they lower their gaze and restrain their sexual passions. That is purer for them. And say to the believing women that they lower their gaze and restrain their sexual passions and do not display their adornment except what appears thereof. And let them wear their head-coverings over their bosoms" (24:30, 31).

With these precautions, women have every liberty to go anywhere they like and to do any work that they like. It should be clearly understood that the veil was only a mark of rank; there is no injunction in the Holy Qur'an or the Hadith requiring women to wear a veil. On the other hand, it is an admitted fact that women joined the prayer service daily in mosques without wearing a veil, while in the pilgrimage they were actually forbidden to wear a veil.

APPENDIX

SUMMARY OF ISLAMIC TEACHINGS

Woman is a free person in the fullest sense of the word, as free as a man. She can earn property (4:32); she can own it and dispose of it as she likes (4:4); she can inherit property, like the male or along with the male heirs (4:7). Spiritually too she stands on a level with the male (3:194; 40:40; 16:97). She is even recognised as being the recipient of Divine revelation (3:41; 28:7).

Marriage relationship is given the same importance as blood relationship (25:54). Marriage serves a double purpose in human society, being the means of the moral uplift of man and of the multiplication of human race (7:189; 30:21; 42:11). Celibate life is against the teachings of the Holy Qur'an which requires every Muslim to live in a married state (24:32). If anyone has not the means, he should try to keep himself chaste by other means (B. 30:10; B. 67:6, 8). Marriage is a sacred contract which a man and a woman enter into by mutual agreement (2:232; 4:21). Temporary marriage is forbidden (B. 64:40). A Muslim may marry a non-Muslim woman (5:5). Marriage is forbidden within certain degrees of relationship (44:23, 24). The rule is the marriage of one man with one woman, but in exceptional cases a man is allowed to take another wife (4:3).

Marriage should be preceded by a proposal (B. 67:37). It is recommended that before making a proposal, a man should satisfy himself as to the desirability of the match (Tr. 9:5). The guardian must obtain the woman's consent for marriage (B. 67:42); where a woman was given in marriage by her father and she disliked the match, the marriage was annulled (B. 67:43). Marriage among equals is recommended, but all Muslims being equal there is no limitation as to the choice of the mate (IM. 9:46). Nobility of character is the most valuable gift of a woman which should be taken into consideration in marrying her (B. 67:16). A dowry must be settled on the woman at the time of marriage, there being no limitation as to its amount (4 :4, 20). The dowry may be increased or decreased by mutual consent after marriage (4 :24). Any conditions may be laid down at the time of marriage, so long as they are not against the law of Islam (B. 54:6). Marriage must be publicly proclaimed, and it is recommended that it should be held in a public place, and announced with the beat of *duff* (Msh. 13:3). The contract is given a sacred character by a sermon before the parties announce their acceptance (AD. 12:31). A feast is recommended when the bride comes to the bridegroom's house (B. 67:72).

Divorce is permitted, but it is stated to be "the most detestable of all things permitted" (AD. 13:3); the right should, therefore, be exercised under exceptional circumstances. When differences between husband and wife arise, every effort should first be made for reconciliation and private judges should be appointed for the purpose (4:35). Divorce may be resorted to only if reconciliation cannot be effected (4:125-130). The wife can claim divorce for any good reason (2:229; Ah. 5, 277), even though there is no ill-treatment on the part of the husband (B. 68:12). Divorce should be pronounced during the period of cleanness (B. 65:65), and should be followed by '*idda*' a waiting period of about three months. During this period, the wife should remain in the house of her husband, and the parties are free to re-establish marital relations (2:228; 67:1). After the waiting period has passed away, the parties may remarry (2:232). But the option for re-establishment of marital relations and remarriage is limited to two occasions (2:229). The dowry settled on the wife at the time of marriage cannot be taken back by the husband on divorce, unless the wife is guilty of adultery (4:20), or she wants a divorce without any fault on the part of the husband (B. 68:12). Divorce should be pronounced only once; its utterance thrice on one occasion is un-Islamic (Ns. 27:6).

Special stress is laid on kindly and good treatment towards the wife. "Keep them in good fellowship or let them go with kindness" (2:229) is a direction which requires kindness towards woman even when she is divorced. And again: "Retain them in good fellowship or set them free with liberality, and do not retain them for injury" (2:231). Kindness is recommended even when a man dislikes his wife: "Treat them kindly; and if you dislike them, it may be that you dislike a thing while Allah has placed abundant good in it" (4:19). Good treatment of the wife is made an index of a man's excellence: "The most excellent of you is he who is best in his treatment of his wife" (Msh. 13:11). Addressing the vast assemblage of people at Makkah, the holy Prophet said in his Farewell Pilgrimage address: "They (your wives) are the trust of Allah in your hands, so you must treat them with all kindness" (M. 15:19).

Much of the happiness of home-life depends on its privacy. Going into houses without permission is strictly forbidden: "Do not enter houses other than your own houses until you have asked permission and saluted their inmates" (24:27). The inside of the house is regarded as a sacred place which can be entered only on permission. A curtain at the door secures the privacy of the inmates, and what is known as *Hijab* or seclusion (32:53) is only another name for this privacy. To ensure happier marital relations, it is recommended that a woman should not be alone in private with a man unless there is present a *dhu-mahram*, a very near relative (B.67:112). For the same reason, too, free mingling of the sexes is discarded. Women have every right to go out of their houses for their needs (B. 4:13; B. 67:116), and there is no seclusion of women in this sense.

But when going out, they are required to be properly dressed; they should not make a display of their finery or uncover certain parts of the body such as the bosom (24:30, 31). The wearing of an overgarment is recommended for this purpose (33:59). What the Islamic social system really prohibits is the displaying of beauty in such a manner as to excite the passions of the other sex; it does not prohibit the going out of women for their needs. The veil or covering of the face was never required by Islam, and women said their prayers in congregation in mosques unveiled. When performing the pilgrimage women were forbidden putting on a veil (B. 25:23). The Holy Prophet is reported to have said to a young woman who was not properly dressed: "When the woman attains her majority, it is not proper that any part of her body should be seen except this and this," and he pointed to his face and his hands (AD. 31:30).

IV

THE STATE

The State was originally intended to ensure liberty and justice for man and protect him from the oppression of his more powerful neighbours, but with the advancement of material civilisation its tendency is more and more to deprive man of his freedom, to enslave him, and to become an instrument of oppression instead of being a check on it. Broadly speaking, material civilisation has developed three kinds of States: the Democratic State, the Fascist State and the Bolshevik State. Of these the Fascist tells us in plain words that the State is all in all, the individual being only a slave to carry out its will. The Fascist leaders are at least candid, though undoubtedly wrong when they say that "the dogma according to which the individual personality has a right to its liberty and to its dignity can bring nothing but destruction," or that "man is only free in and through the whole; the whole can only be a sovereign State which tolerates no discussion and no control." The Bolshevik State, which may rightly be called the Capitalist State, goes a step further than the Fascist and carries to the extreme in practice the Fascist theory by depriving the individual both of his freedom and his property. As regards democracy, its claims are high-sounding so far as the theory goes, but in practice it goes further than even its two younger sisters by enslaving under different names more than half the human race, whose only fault is their weakness.

All these new conceptions of the State are the natural outcome of the lines along which the material civilisation of the West is advancing. Material benefits have so obsessed the views of the civilised world that God and religion have been relegated to the corner of oblivion

THE STATE

and the higher values of life are utterly neglected, not only in Bolshevik Russia where atheism has become the State religion, or in Germany where the Fuehrer is taken for a demi-god, but even in countries which nominally still owe allegiance to Christ and Christianity. The Western States may not be one in their lip professions so far as the supreme authority of God is concerned, but, strangely enough, they are one in worshipping the two new gods which material civilisation has created in place of the One God Whom it has dismissed as a thing of the past. The Nation and the State are the new idols before which the civilised man has fallen prostrate. And along with the old - perhaps the oldest living - god, Mammon, Materialism has its own Trinity in the place of the Trinity of the Church. The gain of economic advantages or the acquisition of wealth being the sole consideration of the civilised man, he is prepared to make any sacrifice that is required of him to gain this end, in the name of the State and for the love of the Nation. Wealth, Nation and the State have thus the highest place of honour in the heart of the civilised man and he worships these idols. The desire to bow is there in human nature, and if men will not bow before their Maker, they must bow before things of their own making. Objects unworthy of worship have, however, always led humanity to ruin, and the worship of Mammon and its two associates, the Nation and the State, through which alone access can be had to the chief idol of the Trinity of Materialism, is even now leading civilisation to sure destruction.

The State was needed to stop the aggression of man against man, to protect the weak against the strong and to ensure justice between man and man. But where do we find the civilised State? The State in the West, whether it is labelled as a Democracy or as a Fascist or a Bolshevik State, stands for expansion, for aggression and for oppressing the weak who are considered to be unfit to take care of themselves. It is not Machiavelli alone with whom "consideration of justice or injustice" carries no weight, and "every scruple must be set aside" when the safety of the

State is at stake. Even those who condemn him are following in his footsteps; they go in fact a step further, as the expansion of the State is as much of a duty with them as its defence. With the gold of the world in their possession and with their bombs and bombers, they claim that they have got an additional right of expanding themselves to bring more and more economic advantages to their own people. Marching into another nation's country becomes a duty with them when that nation is too weak to defend itself; falling on it like a bolt from the blue so that it should not be able to take any measures of self-defence is a happy performance. Aggression is the very essence of the civilised State. The weak have no rights; the right belongs to those who have the might, who have the strength to command respect and attention; so that if a weak neighbour does not pay attention to the word of a powerful State, it may be wiped out of its existence. This mentality has been developed by every Western nation, so that every State strives to outvie others in its armies and armaments. And the result is the deadly conflict of the different States and a burning passion to destroy one another.

The responsibility for this state of things rests entirely with the materialistic conception of the State. Every State must necessarily be invested with power with which it may stop aggression and oppression and protect the weak, dealing out fair justice to all. The advance of science has increased this power thousandfold. On the other hand, materialistic outlook on life has made man more unscrupulous in the use of his power against fellow-man, and with the advancement in the conquest of Nature, the conquest of self, which alone serves as a check on the tyranny of man against man, has been retarded and thrown to the background. The result is that the increased powers of the State which must necessarily be exercised through individuals are being used more for the enslavement and destruction of man than for his deliverance from tyranny and for upholding the cause of truth and justice. It has been rightly remarked that while science has given man powers fit for the gods, to their use, the civilised man brings the mentality of a savage. The State, instead of being helpful in increasing human happiness for which it was originally meant, has become the greatest menace to human happiness, the individual being so enthralled by this idol that, willingly or unwillingly, he is working as part of a machinery for the destruction of humanity.

It is to remedy this evil that Islam requires the vesting of State authority in the hands of men who are God-fearing before all. The head of the State in Islam is called both an Amir, (lit. *one who commands*) and an Imam, (lit. *a person whose example is followed*), i.e. a person who stands on a very high moral plane. On his death-bed, the Holy Prophet gave an indication as to who should succeed him as the head of the Muslim State by appointing Abu Bakr, admittedly the fittest man, to lead prayers for the Muslims in his absence. For a long time this practice was continued, and the head of the State led the prayers. Righteousness -- fear of God and regard for other people's rights -- was as necessary a qualification for the ruler as fitness to rule. Spiritual force alone could enable a man to control the powers which temporal authority gives him, and which in the absence of such a force are often in danger of being abused. The early Islamic State organisation, which combined the offices of the spiritual and the temporal head of the community, was, therefore, the most perfect which the history of statecraft can show. The head of the State considered himself responsible to God, in the first place, for the exercise of his temporal authority. His responsibility to those who elected him was secondary.

There exists a misconception in some quarters that the Islamic State was a theocracy. The head of the Muslim State never considered himself a representative of God on earth but a representative of men who was chosen to serve them, but he certainly considered himself responsible to God for every act that he did in the exercise of his authority. Perhaps history cannot show a greater conqueror than 'Umar, the second successor of the Holy Prophet, a conqueror and an administrator at one and the same time. Yet he would not stop even one of his lowest subjects rebuking him in public. "Fear God, O 'Umar!" said the man repeatedly; and when some people wanted to stop the man, 'Umar himself intervened, saying, "Let him say so; of what use are these people if they do not tell me such things?" This monarch of four kingdoms visited a famine-stricken camp at night *incognito*, and when he found a woman with no food to give her children he rushed back to Madinah, a distance of three miles, and took a sack of flour on his back to feed the destitute woman and her children. When a servant offered his services to carry the load, he simply replied: "In this life you might carry my burden for me, but who will carry my burden on the Day of Judgement?" Yet when this great servant of his people was lying on his death-bed and a young man lauded his great services, he said: "Enough, young fellow! it is sufficient if the evil I may have done in the exercise of authority is neutralised by any good that I have done." It is such a mental attitude alone which can make men fit for ruling their fellow-beings. But such a mentality is created only by a strong faith in God and a feeling of one's responsibility to God.

It was such a responsible government that Islam created, a government by men who realised that above all other things they were responsible to God for every thing which they did. Then men to be honoured -- and entrusting a man with command was certainly doing him honour -- were those who paid the greatest regard to their duties (49:13), and it was such men that were to be placed in authority over others: "Allah commands you to make over (positions of) trust to those worthy of them" (4:58). Everyone who was entrusted with authority in the State organisation was told that he was a ruler in his own sphere, and that he was responsible to God for those who were placed under his trust: "Everyone of you is a ruler and everyone of you shall be questioned about those under his rule; the king is a ruler and he shall be questioned about his subjects; and the man is a ruler in his family and he shall be questioned about those under his care; and the woman is a ruler in the house of her husband and she shall be questioned about those under her care; and the servant is a ruler so far as the property of his master is concerned and he shall be questioned about that which is entrusted to him" (B. 11:11). The ruler or head of the State is thus, along with all those persons who hold any authority over others, placed in the same category as a servant. Just as a servant is entrusted with a certain property for which he is responsible to his master, those entrusted with State authority, in whatever position they may be, are entrusted with the care of the people and guarding their rights, and for the proper discharge of their duties they are responsible, in the first place, to the real Master Who is God, and then to the people who have entrusted them with this charge. A right mentality of the different parts of the State machinery is the first necessity of a good State organisation, and the greatest stress is therefore laid on this in the Islamic conception of the State.

The verses and the hadith quoted above show further that hereditary kingship is foreign to the conception of the State in Islam. Nor is it an autocracy, as uncontrolled authority is not vested in the head of the State. Speaking of the great qualities of Muslims, their reliance on their God, their shunning of all kinds of indecency, their forgiveness, their keeping up of prayers, the Holy Qur'an says: "And their rule is by counsel among themselves" (42:38). So much so was the principle of counsel to be adhered to that the Holy Prophet himself was enjoined to take counsel with his followers in affairs of State: "Pardon them and ask protection for them and take counsel with them in affairs of the State" (3:158). The Islamic State is thus a democracy in the truest sense of the word. The first successor to the Holy Prophet was Abu Bakr who was elected as the head of the State by the agreement of all parties, and so were the three successors that followed him.

Why the State organisation was needed and what the constitutional position of the head of the State was, was explained by Abu Bakr in his very first address:

"You have elected me as *Khalifa* (successor to the Holy Prophet as temporal head of the State), but I claim no superiority over you. The strongest among you shall be the weakest with me until I get the rights of others from him, and the weakest among you shall be the strongest with me until I get all his rights......Help me if I act rightly and correct me if I take a wrong course.....Obey me so long as I obey God and his Messenger. In case I disobey God and His Messenger, I have no right to obedience from you."

The people's responsibility to the State is to respect its laws and obey its orders so long as they do not require disobedience to God and His Messenger; orders of the State which involved disobedience to God shall not be obeyed (B. 56:108). It was considered an act of great merit, "an excellent *Jihad*", to speak out the truth in the presence of an unjust ruler (M<u>sh</u>. 17). But active opposition to constituted authority or rebellion against it is not allowed, "unless you see an act of open unbelief in which you have a clear argument from Allah" (B. 93:2). In such an extreme case, the *Khalifa* may even be deposed. The head of the State was a servant of the State who was paid a fixed salary for maintenance out of the public treasury, like all other public servants. He had no special privileges, and in his private capacity he could be sued in the court like any other member of the Muslim community. The great 'Umar, ruler of four kingdoms, appeared as a defendant in the court of a magistrate. Among the orders given to his provincial governors was this that they shall be accessible at all hours of the day to those who had a complaint to make, and that they shall not keep a doorkeeper who should prohibit people from approaching them. And further that they shall make themselves accustomed to lead hard lives. The head of the State carried on the administration with the help of ministers, all important State affairs being decided by a council.

Those entrusted with carrying on the work of governments, including the head, were required to work for the good of the people: "There is not a man whom Allah grants to rule people, then he does not manage their affairs for their good but he will not smell the sweet odour of paradise" (B. 94:8). They were required to be gentle to the people, so as to make them rejoice on account of the State Management, and were forbidden to do anything which might cause aversion (B. 64:62). They were enjoined to lead simple lives and to be easily accessible to those who needed their services (Msh. 17:1), to be God-fearing (B. 94:16), to tax the different classes of people according to their capacity, to provide for those who could not earn and to have as much regard for the rights of the non-Muslims as for those of the Muslims (B. 62:8). The State was not only required to maintain uncared-for families, but also to pay the unpaid debts which were contracted for a lawful need (B. 43:11).

As regards relations with other States and questions of peace and war, the motto of the Islamic State is *a defensive war* and *a generous peace*. War was a necessary human condition but the principle was laid down in the clearest words that there should be no aggression. It was in defence alone that permission was granted to the Muslims to fight: "And fight in the way of Allah with those who fight with you and do not exceed this limit" (2:190). And on another occasion: "Permission (to fight) is given to those on whom war is made, because they are oppressed" (22:39).

This does not leave the slightest doubt that Islam does not allow aggressive war; neither does it allow a war for expansion, nor a war for prestige. It only allows war when a State has been attacked. And even then, if the enemy offers peace, peace must be concluded. The enemies of Islam attacked the Muslim State to annihilate it. "They will not cease fighting with you," says the Holy Qur'an, "until they turn you back from your religion, if they can" (2:217). Yet even if such an enemy desired peace, the Muslim State could not refuse it. "If they incline to peace, incline thou also to it, and trust in Allah" (8:61). The proposal of peace might be insincere; it might be made to gain time and prepare for another war; but even then peace was to be preferred: "And if they intend to deceive thee, then surely Allah is sufficient for thee" (8:62). The Muslim's faith in Allah was an assurance to him that if the enemy made another war, he would again be defeated and would have to beg for peace.

Such a war was a mercy; it was mercy at its start because it had to be fought in self-defence -- the people were to be saved from an aggressor who was out to annihilate them; it was a mercy in the end because it had to be stopped when the aggressor sued for peace -- safety of the oppressed and not the annihilation of the aggressor, being the object. It was a mercy for the non-combatants, who in civilised warfare are greater victims of the tyranny of war than even the combatants, as there was an express prohibition against the killing of non-combatants (B. 56:147). Not even the aggressors were to be annihilated, because annihilation was not the only means of stopping the aggression. At times, a generous peace was a better corrective than annihilation. The attempt to annihilate a people would only fan the fire of revenge among the vanquished, while a generous peace might bring about a change of heart. Hence it was that Islam did not allow the rejection of an offer of peace even by an aggressor.

It was in this generous spirit that the Holy Prophet treated his own enemies. For twenty-one long years he suffered unimaginable tortures at the hands of his foes; he and his band of faithful followers were persecuted most cruelly: even when they fled from their homes and found a haven of peace in distant Madinah, the powerful warriors of Makkah attacked them in their new homes. Three times did the enemy attack Madinah with strong forces to annihilate the small Muslim community that had found shelter there. Yet when the time came to punish the brutal aggressors who were at the mercy of the Holy Prophet and his followers at the conquest of Makka, they were greeted with a message of love: "This day there shall be no reproach against you." This generous treatment brought about a change of heart in the erstwhile blood-thirsty enemies, turning them into fast friends. It is such a peace that the world needs to-day, but only a State based on the broad principles of Islam could offer such a peace.

There exists a great misconception regarding *jihad*, one of the five basic religious obligations of a Muslim. It literally means *the exerting of one's power in repelling the enemy* or *in contending with an object of disapprobation*. In the terminology of Islam, it is used in both these senses, being applied to the purely missionary activities of a Muslim and his defence of the faith in a physical sense. The first duty, the duty to invite people to Islam, is a permanent duty laid upon all Muslims of all ages, while the second is a duty which arises upon certain contingencies. The Holy Qur'an and the Hadith call attention to both these duties in the clearest and most forceful words, under the name of *jihad*. A Jihad -- *Jihad-an kabiran*, or a *mighty struggle* -- by means of the Qur'an must be carried on against the unbelievers, we are told: "Strive hard against them (*jahid-hum*) a mighty striving (*jihad-an kabir-an*) with it (*i.e.*, the Qur'an)" (25:52). Islam's greatest *jihad* is, therefore, not by means of the sword but by means of the Holy Qur'an, *i.e.* a missionary effort to carry the message of Islam to all nations. Hence it is laid down that there should always be among Muslims a party to invite people to Islam: "And from among you there should be a party who invite to good and enjoin the right and forbid the wrong. And these are they who are successful" (3:103).

Fighting was undoubtedly allowed but it was expressly allowed only as a defensive measure against those who took up the sword to annihilate Islam, as already shown. The sword could not be used to force Islam on others, compulsion in religion being forbidden in clear words: "There is no compulsion in religion" (2:256). There is not a single instance on record in the Holy Prophet's life in which an expedition was undertaken to convert a people to Islam; nor was a single individual ever required to confess the faith of Islam at the point of the sword. Speaking of the fighting with Iran in 'Umar's time, and quoting 'Umar as saying: "I desire that between Mesopotamia and the countries beyond the hills shall be a barrier so that the Persians shall not be able to get at us, nor we at them," even Muir admits that "the obligation to enforce Islam by a universal crusade had not yet dawned upon the Muslim mind." If such an idea was unknown to Muslim mind in the life-time of the Holy Prophet or during the Early Caliphate, it certainly is not Islamic.